Weird Science

40 Strange-Acting, Bizarre-Looking, and Barely Believable Activities for Kids

Jim Wiese

Illustrations by Ed Shems

JOSSEY-BASS
A Wiley Imprint
www.josseybass.com

For Jeremy and Mike,
friends who help make teaching science
both weird and wonderful

Published by Jossey-Bass
A Wiley Imprint
989 Market Street, San Francisco, CA 94103-1741   www.josseybass.com

Published simultaneously in Canada

Design and production by Navta Associates, Inc.

Jossey-Bass books and products are available through most bookstores. To contact Jossey-Bass directly call our Customer Care Department within the U.S. at 800-956-7739, outside the U.S. at 317-572-3986, or fax 317-572-4002.

Jossey-Bass also publishes its books in a variety of electronic formats. Some content that appears in print may not be available in electronic books.

Library of Congress Cataloging-in-Publication Data

Wiese, Jim, date.
Weird science : 40 strange-acting, bizarre-looking, and barely believable activities for kids / Jim Wiese ; illustrations by Ed Shems.
    p. cm.
Includes index.
ISBN 0-471-46229-2 (paper : alk. paper)
1. Science—Experiments—Juvenile literature. I. Shems, Ed., ill. II. Title.
Q164.W5345 2004
507'.8—dc22

                                                                2004002280

Printed in the United States of America
FIRST EDITION
PB Printing   10 9 8 7 6 5 4 3

CONTENTS

ACKNOWLEDGMENTS

The idea for this book came from my editor, Kate Bradford. She suggested I write an outline for a book tentatively titled *Weird Science*. Just the title made ideas swirl inside my head. What exactly does weird science mean? Weird things can make you say, "Wow," "Huh?" or "Oh, gross." Almost everything in science seems weird to me in one way or another—weird, wonderful, and almost unbelievable! But mostly I've found weird science to be memorable. As a teacher I'd used stories of weird things in science, from dry ice to the shape of a red blood cell, to motivate my students, who have told me that these stories were one of the things they most remembered from my classes. With that in mind, I started to talk to other science teachers about what their students found weird. My family, friends, and colleagues were quick to tell me what they found weird, and the outline for the book took shape. A special thanks to all those who gave me weird ideas and shared their thoughts.

As always, I would like to thank the team of people at John Wiley & Sons who worked to make this book a reality. At the center is the work of my editor, Kate Bradford. Her continued professionalism in every aspect of the publishing process brings out the best in my writing. Thanks for this great idea.

INTRODUCTION

Have you ever heard a news report about ball lightning or the aurora borealis and wondered what they were talking about? Do you know about some weird plants and animals, like insect eating plants and naked mole rats? Is dry ice really dry? Is a slime mold really slimy? Is quicksand really quick? If you've ever asked yourself these questions, and more, but don't know where to begin to find the answers, *Weird Science* is the place to start. Science is behind many different things that at first seem really weird. But the more you understand about the science behind weird stuff, the more interesting it becomes. So get ready for over 40 exciting activities that will let you learn more about things that are unusual, weird, and bizarre.

How to Use This Book

This book is divided into chapters based on types of weird things: weird substances, weird plants, weird animals, weird microbes, weird weather, weird Earth, weird sights, weird sounds, and weird physics. In each chapter there are projects that teach you about the science that's behind the phenomena. Each project has a list of materials and a procedure to follow. You'll be able to find most of the materials needed around the house or at your neighborhood hardware, or grocery store. Some of the projects have a section called *More Fun Stuff to Do,* which lets you try different variations on the original activity. Explanations are given at the end of each group of projects. Words in **bold** type are defined in the glossary at the back of the book.

Being a Good Scientist

- Read through the instructions once completely before you start the activity or experiment.

- Collect all the equipment you'll need before you start the activity or experiment.

- If possible, keep a notebook. Write down what you do in your experiment or project and what happens.

- Follow the instructions carefully. *Do not attempt to do yourself any steps that require the help of an adult.*

- If your experiment or project does not work properly the first time, try again or try doing it in a slightly different way. In real life, experiments don't always work out perfectly the first time.

- Always have an open mind that asks questions and looks for answers. The basis of good science is asking good questions and finding the best answers.

Increasing Your Understanding

- Make small changes in the design of the equipment or project to see if the results stay the same. Change only one thing at a time so you can tell which change caused a particular result.

- Make up an experiment or activity to test your own ideas about how things work.

- Look at the things around you for examples of the scientific principles that you have learned.

- Don't worry if at first you don't understand the things around you. There are always new things to discover. Remember that many of the most famous discoveries were made by accident.

Using This Book to Do a Science Fair Project

Many of the activities in this book can serve as the starting point for a science fair project. After doing the experiment as it is written in the book, what questions come to mind? Some possible projects are suggested in the section of the activities called "More Fun Stuff to Do."

To begin your science fair project, you will first need to write down the problem you want to study and come up with a hypothesis. A **hypothesis** is an educated guess about the results of an experiment you are going to perform. For example, if you enjoyed the Quicksand activity, you may want to find out if other substances will do the same thing. A hypothesis for this experiment could be that all white powders will make a mixture that seems to be both solid and liquid. Next you will have to devise an experiment to test your hypothesis. In the Quicksand example, you might mix several different white powders, such as baking soda, flour or sugar, with a small amount of water, then observe and record the results. You can then compare these results to what you got when you mixed cornstarch with water. Be sure to keep careful records of your experiment. Next you will analyze the data you recorded. In the Quicksand example, you could create a table showing the names of the substances you tested and how they reacted. For some experiments, a graph is a good way to show your results. Finally, you should come up with a conclusion that shows how your results prove or disprove your hypothesis.

This process is called the **scientific method.** When following the scientific method, you begin with a hypothesis, test it with an experiment, analyze the results, and draw a conclusion.

A Word of Warning

Some science experiments can be dangerous. *Ask an adult to help you with experiments that call for adult help, such as those that involve matches, knives, or other sharp instruments.* Don't forget to ask permission to use household items, and put away your equipment and clean up your work area when you have finished experimenting. Good scientists are careful and avoid accidents.

WEIRD SUBSTANCES
Slip, Ooze, and Creep

We've all been told that there are three states, or phases, of matter—solid, liquid, and gas. **Solids** have a distinct, fixed volume and well-defined shape. A piece of ice is a solid. **Liquids** also have a fixed volume, but they have no shape of their own. They take the shape of the container they are in. Water is a liquid. Finally come gases. **Gases** have no fixed volume or shape so they take the shape and volume of the container they are in. Water vapor is a gas. It all seems so simple.

But science is never that easy. While the distinction between solid, liquid, and gas is easy to grasp, what about substances that don't really fit into those categories? There are some weird substances out there that can act like both liquids and solids. There are also common substances, such as water, that can act pretty weird sometimes, too. Try the activities in this chapter to learn more about the weird substances around you.

 **PROJECT 1**

Slime

While most substances are solids, liquids or gases, some slimy things are substances that don't really fit our usual states of matter.

To learn more about slime, how about making some? Try this activity to learn how.

Materials

newspaper
measuring spoon
borax powder (available in the
    detergent section of your grocery
    store)
2 8-ounce glass jars
measuring cup
distilled water

small sticks (for stirring)
food coloring
4-ounce bottle of white glue
    (Elmer's Glue works best—
    don't ask me why)
yogurt container, washed and
    dried
resealable plastic bag

Caution: Do not get the slimy substance you create in this activity onto your clothes or the furniture.

Procedure

1. Spread the newspaper on the table. This activity can get messy.

2. Place ½ teaspoon (2.5 ml) of borax into one of the jars.

3. Add 1 cup of distilled water to the borax in the jar.

4. Use a stick to mix the borax in the water until it dissolves.

5. Placc one drop of food coloring, 1 cup of distilled water, and the glue into the other jar. Use another stick to mix these substances together.

6. Pour about half the contents of each jar into the yogurt container. Mix the substances until the mixture has a nice gooey feel.

7. Touch the substance with your finger. Is it a solid or a liquid? Put some in your hand. How does it feel now?

More Fun Stuff to Do

Try making slime using different colors of food coloring.

Explanation

The slimy substance that you created in this experiment is not quite a liquid and not quite a solid. In the 1700s, Isaac Newton named the properties of most fluids. However, Newton's explanations work best for pure substances, like water. These are called **Newtonian fluids.**

But other substances are not pure, and when you mix them together they don't obey the usual rules. These are called **non-Newtonian fluids.** The slime you mixed in this activity is a non-Newtonian fluid. Sometimes it seems like a solid and sometimes it seems like a liquid.

Quicksand

Besides slime, there are other substances that seem to be caught between being a solid and a liquid. You may have seen one in the movies. An explorer is traveling through the jungle when he suddenly falls into a pit that appears to be filled with some kind of mushy liquid. Too late he realizes he's fallen into quicksand. Slowly he gets pulled under by the goopy muck. But is this actually what would happen? And what kind of a substance is quicksand?

To learn more, try the next activity to make another non-Newtonian fluid and learn how it relates to quicksand.

Materials

measuring cups
¼ cup (65 ml) cornstarch
clear plastic cup
¼ cup tap water
spoon

Procedure

1. Put the cornstarch in the plastic cup.

2. Add the tap water, a little at a time, to the cornstarch. Stir the mixture with the spoon. *Note: Be careful not to add too much water. The mixture should be very thick.*

3. Pour about a tablespoon (15 ml) of the white liquid into one of your hands. The liquid will pour very easily from the cup.

4. Touch the liquid with a finger of your other hand, and then remove your finger. Can you explain what happened?

Explanation

When you touch the cornstarch mixture it instantly turns hard. It then turns back into a liquid.

Matter takes the form of solid, liquid, or gas. However, solids, liquids, and gases can be mixed together in interesting ways. When one substance dissolves or disappears completely into another, the result is called a **solution.** The cornstarch and water mixture is not a solution, however, it is a slightly different kind of mixture called a colloid. A **colloid** is a mixture of tiny particles of one substance scattered evenly throughout another. In this case, the cornstarch particles are scattered evenly throughout the water.

Colloids can change form under pressure. In this activity, when the mixture is in the cup it appears to be a liquid. But when you touch the solution, the touch puts pressure on the mixture. The pressure forces the cornstarch particles together and the mixture shifts to a solid form. When the pressure is released, the mixture returns to its original liquid form. The scientific term for this kind of non-Newtonian fluid is **thixotropic,** which means changes through the act of handling.

Weird Science IN ACTION

Quicksand is really not any special kind of sand. It's actually something that happens when regular sand is surrounded by a thin film of water so that the sand particles don't touch each other. Often it happens when there is a constant underground flow of water into a sandy area, such as with an underground spring. The movement of the water causes the individual grains of sand to separate from one another and a thin layer of water to move between each grain. The water decreases the friction between the grains of sand so they move more easily. The water isn't strong enough to completely move the grains of sand apart, so it still looks like solid ground. But when someone steps in the soupy pool of sand and water, the sand particles move apart and the person is stuck in the quicksand.

In spite of what you may have seen in the movies, most patches of quicksand are shallow, only a few inches deep. And quicksand does not suck its victims down to their death. It's actually more like trying to swim in really thick vegetable soup. Since quicksand is sand and water, it's more dense than the human body and if you remain calm, you can float in it. (Actually you would float higher in it than in pure water.) Some people have been known to swim to safety using a dog-paddling stroke, while others simply move very slowly to push themselves to shore. If you move too quickly or thrash about in the quicksand, you can find yourself moving under the quicksand. Then it's more difficult to get out because of the weight of the sand above you.

Curved Water

PROJECT 3

When you look at water in a glass, at first glance it appears to have a level surface. But if you look closer, you'll see that not all the water is on the level. Try this activity to learn more about the weird behavior of curved water.

Materials

tall, narrow glass jar (like one that is used to hold olives), clean and dried with label removed

water

paper towel

penny

eyedropper

Procedure

1. Fill the glass jar half full of water and put it on a table or counter.

2. Bend down so that your eye is at the same level as the top of the water in the jar.

3. Look at the surface of the water near the middle of the jar and then near the edges, where the water touches the glass jar. What do you see? What does the water do near the glass surface?

4. Lay a piece of paper towel on the table. Place the penny flat in the middle of the paper towel.

5. Use the eyedropper to place a drop of water on the top of the penny. What happens?

6. Continue to add several more drops of water to the top of the penny. What happens to the surface of the water?

More Fun Stuff to Do

Keep adding drops of water carefully to the top of the penny. How many drops of water can you add before the water spills off the penny?

Explanation

If you look carefully at the water's surface where it comes in contact with the glass jar, you'll notice that the water curves up near the glass. You will also notice that the drops of water on the top of the penny will form a curved surface and you'll be able to put many more drops of water on the penny than you might have expected.

Water is influenced by the force of gravity and, for the most part, will form a flat surface when given the chance. But there are other forces that can act on water as well. Water is made of **molecules** (particles made up of two or more atoms). Molecules of some substances, such as water molecules, are attracted to each other. They are called polar molecules. One end of each molecule of water has a positive charge and the other end has a negative charge.

This difference in charge creates another force, an electromagnetic force, that creates a special property of water called **surface tension.** The positive part of one molecule is attracted to the negative part of another. Each water molecule is attracted in all directions to the water molecules that surround it. The surface of the glass is also electrically charged, so when a water molecule is near the glass, it is attracted to it. This includes the glass that is slightly above the surface of the water, so the water is pulled up near the edges, creating a curved surface.

This surface tension is also behind the curved water surface on the top of the penny. Molecules on the surface of water have no molecules above them, so they are only attracted to those next to and underneath them. This attraction creates a tension like a thin skin on the surface of the water. The surface tension of water can be strong enough to overcome the force of gravity. Adding more water makes the drop grow larger, but the surface tension of the drop holds it together like a small water balloon. It will keep getting larger until the force of gravity is greater than the surface tension of the drop and the water spills over the edge of the penny.

Weird Science IN ACTION

The surface tension of water plays an important part in some insects' lives. It lets them walk on water! Some insects that live near the water, such as the water strider, can skate and jump on the surface of the water. They use this ability to catch other, smaller water insects that they eat for dinner. The backswimmer is another insect that uses water surface tension, but in a backwards way. It can hang upside-down in the water, hanging from the water's surface. It uses this unusual ability to lay in wait for other small water insects to swim by. Like the water strider, the backswimmer captures and eats smaller water insects.

Another place where water's attraction to the surface that holds it is at work is in the thin tubes inside plants called xylem. These tubes let water flow from the roots to the leaves. There are several different ways that water moves up from a plant's roots. One of the things that moves the water is **capillary action,** a special name given to the movement of water through or along very thin tubes due to the attraction of the water to the sides of the tubes. It is one of the forces that lets water travel more than 300 feet (100 m) up to the tops of the tallest trees, the redwoods.

Dry Ice

When you hear the word "ice," you probably think about the cubes of solid water that you put in your summer drinks to make them colder. But there is another kind of ice. It's called dry ice and is made from the gas we normally exhale, carbon dioxide (CO_2). While it may share the same name as its water-based cousin, it acts more like a distant relative with weird actions. So, try these activities to learn more about dry ice.

Materials

paper towel
ice cube
winter gloves
dry ice (available from many ice
   companies)
modeling clay

aluminum pie tin
candle
matches
glass
water
adult helper

Caution: Have an adult supervise when you're using dry ice. Never touch the dry ice with your bare hands. Always wear winter gloves when touching or moving the dry ice. Always use dry ice in a well ventilated room.

Procedure

1. Place the paper towel on the table in front of you.

2. Place the ice cube on the paper towel.

3. Put on the winter gloves and place a small piece of dry ice on the paper towel.

4. Watch the two kinds of ice. What happens to each as they warm up?

5. Place a small ball of modeling clay in the bottom of the pie tin.

6. Stick the candle in the middle of the modeling clay so that the candle sits upright in the center of the pie tin.

7. Have an adult help you light the candle with a match.

8. Pour some water into the glass. With the winter gloves on, place a piece of dry ice in the glass of water. What happens?

9. Hold the glass about 6 inches (15 cm) above the candle flame so that the gases escaping from the glass fall onto the flame. What happens to the flame?

More Fun Stuff to Do

Try placing dry ice in water of different temperatures. How does it react when placed in cold and hot water?

Explanation

An ice cube will become water when it melts, but when dry ice melts, it turns into a gas. When dry ice is placed in water, it will begin to bubble. When the bubbles reach the surface, a visible gas is released, which goes over the side of the glass. When the gas meets a candle flame, the flame will go out. Warm water will produce more vapor than cool water.

Dry ice is frozen carbon dioxide (CO_2). Dry ice is extremely cold, about $-109°$ F ($-78°$ C). Carbon dioxide is usually a gas at normal temperatures. We exhale carbon dioxide and it makes up about 35 percent of our atmosphere gases. At normal temperatures, frozen carbon dioxide doesn't melt into a liquid, but evaporates directly into its gas form. That's why it's called dry ice—it never gets wet! This process of going from a solid directly to a gas is called **sublimation.**

When dry ice is placed in water, it changes from its solid form into a gas. As this happens, the carbon dioxide expands, forming bubbles on the surface of the solid dry ice. These bubbles rise to the surface of the water and are released into the air. You see this as a fog. However, this fog is not the carbon dioxide but condensed water vapor mixed with the invisible carbon dioxide gas. Because the change from a solid to a gas depends on the temperature, the warmer the water, the faster the change.

Because carbon dioxide molecules are heavier than the molecules of nitrogen and oxygen in the atmosphere, the gas will move down after leaving the glass. The candle flame needs oxygen to burn. When the carbon dioxide gas reaches the flame, it takes the place of the oxygen around the flame and the fire goes out.

Weird Science IN ACTION

The weird properties of dry ice that you experimented with in this activity have other uses. The visible fog that you formed can be used in movies and television to create a spooky-looking ground fog or to make a magic potion look extra creepy. The extreme cold of the carbon dioxide as it changes from solid to gas causes the water vapor to condense into clouds. Because the fog is heavier than the air around, it will spill out of a container and settle to the ground.

Slime Molds

Later in this book, you'll read about some weird animals, plants, and even bacteria, but there are other strange critters that don't fit into any of these categories. One example is the slime mold. At some times in its life, it acts like a fungus, producing spores to reproduce. But at other times it acts like an amoeba (a single-celled organism that moves by changing its shape).

Slime molds are often difficult to find, so to learn more about them, you'll need to get them from a specialty store. Try this activity to see how weird they really are.

Materials

Slime Mold Growing Kit – (you can order these from a science store, such as Carolina Biological Supply Company [www. carolina.com]; kit includes a single plate culture of Physarum polycephalum, petri dishes, agar, and sterilized oatmeal.)
clean, sharp knife
plastic tape
aluminum foil
magnifying glass

Caution: Molds should not be handled around people who have allergies to them. Dispose of molds properly when finished.

Procedure

These instructions may vary depending on the type of slime mold kit you purchase.

1. Mix the 2 % non-nutrient agar according to the instructions in the kit. (To make 2 % agar mix 20 grams of agar in a liter of distilled water.)

2. Pour the 2 % agar into the bottom half of a petri dish set. Set it aside until it hardens.

3. Sprinkle 15 to 20 flakes of unflavored oatmeal on the agar surface.

4. Use the knife to cut a ½-inch (1-cm) cube of the Physarum polycephalum from the culture provided in the kit.

5. Place the cube near the center of the agar with the Physarum side down.

6. Put the top on the petri dish, then seal the edges with plastic tape.

7. Cover the dish with aluminum foil and set aside. Physarum grows best in the dark, at room temperature.

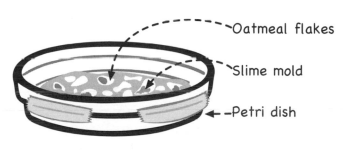

Oatmeal flakes

Slime mold

Petri dish

8. After three days, remove the foil and observe the slime mold. Use the magnifying glass to get a better look. What do you see?

More Fun Stuff to Do

There are many things you can investigate with slime molds.

- Try this activity again, only this time place only two or three oatmeal flakes in the agar. What does the slime mold do?

- Try this activity again, only this time cover only half of the petri dish with aluminum foil. Where does the slime mold grow?

- Try this activity again, only this time grow it at a different temperature. What effect does temperature have on the slime mold's growth?

Explanation

After three days, the Physarum slime mold will begin to grow, engulfing the oatmeal flakes. If you place only a few oatmeal flakes in the agar, the slime mold will sense where it is and only grow in that direction. It will also only grow in the dark and will grow faster in warmer temperatures than in cooler temperatures

When you looked at the slime mold with the magnifying glass, you may have seen thin, threadlike fibers with small balls at the end. These are the sporagiophores (thin fibers) and sporagium (small balls) that they use to reproduce. The sporagium produce spores, which are similar to seeds and can produce a new slime mold.

In this activity, you grew a slime mold known as Physarum poly-cephalum. Slime molds were once considered to be fungi because of their spore reproduction, but unlike other fungi, their **cell membranes** (the stuff that surrounds their cells) don't contain **chitin,** a hard substance that some insect shells are made of. But most important, slime molds can move!

Slime molds are made up of individual cells that form a large, slimy mass. In this state, they sometimes look like blobs, spilled jelly or even dog vomit! They can be bright orange, red, yellow, brown, black, blue, or white. These large masses act like a giant amoeba. As the mass moves along, it engulfs food particles, like the oatmeal flakes you placed on the agar. If you cut up a slime mold, the pieces will pull themselves back together. These slime blobs can move, avoid objects in their way, move toward dark areas, and seem to be able to sense when food is nearby and move toward it.

But how can a slime mold move? Plasmodial slime molds (the most common kind) share one big cell wall that surrounds thousands or millions of cell nuclei. Proteins called **microfilaments** act like tiny muscles that let the slimy mass crawl along the ground at a rate of about $\frac{1}{25}$th of an inch per hour (.1 cm per hour).

When there isn't enough food or water, the plasmodial slime will separate into smaller blobs that form threadlike stalks topped by spherical bodies that contain spores. These spores are carried by wind or rain to new locations where they start new slime molds.

Don't be worried about slime molds in the wild because they eat decaying vegetation, bacteria, fungi, and even other slime molds. They don't eat humans! They are most commonly found in forests and occasionally on grasses or garden mulch.

Weird Science IN ACTION

Cellular slime molds start out as single cells. But these cells are both special and weird. They can give off chemicals that let them communicate with each other. When the chemical message is sent, the cellular slime molds will move together into a tiny sluglike organism that continues to grow and turns into the slime mold that you can see.

Moving "Lava"

PROJECT

In the 1960s, a new fad became a regular feature in college dorms and teenager's bedrooms all over the world. That fad was the "lava lamp," a device that had a light in its base and gooey, colored blobs of liquid moving up and down in a clear or contrasting-colored fluid. You can still find these lamps in some novelty stores and catalogs. The effect is weird as the colored globs slowly move from the bottom of the other fluid to the surface, only to return to the bottom of the container where the journey begins again.

But how can you get one liquid to move up and down while suspended in another? Try this activity to learn one way it can be done.

Materials

2-cup (500-ml) plastic bottle with lid (clean and dry)
measuring cup
water
food coloring
measuring spoon
cooking oil
table salt

Procedure

1. Fill the bottle ¾ full of water.

2. Add 2 drops of food coloring to the water.

3. Swirl the bottle to evenly mix the food coloring in the water.

4. Add 2 tablespoons (30 ml) of cooking oil to the bottle.

5. Wait for several minutes until the oil and water separate. You should get two layers, oil on top and water below it.

6. Pour ⅔ tablespoon (10 ml) of salt into the bottle.

7. Watch the liquids in the bottle. What happens to the oil and water?

More Fun Stuff to Do

Try adding another ⅔ tablespoon (10 ml) of salt. What happens this time? How much salt can you add before the action stops?

Explanation

After you add the salt to the bottle, drops of oil on the surface will begin to sink to the bottom of the bottle where they will come to rest. After a short time, the oil drop will move back up to the surface and remix with the other oil that is there.

When you mix water and oil, as you did in the first part of this activity, you will notice that they don't stay mixed. That is because oil is not soluble in water. When a substance is **soluble,** it will dissolve in other liquid. Since oil and water don't mix, the oil will rest on top of the water because it has a lower density than the water. **Density** is a physical property of matter that is determined by dividing the mass of an object by its volume. When two liquids with different densities are put together, the one with the lower density will float on the surface of the substance with the higher density.

When you added salt to the bottle, the salt sticks to the oil and the density of the salt-and-oil drops becomes higher than the density of the water below it. The drops of salt and oil therefore move from the surface to the bottom of the bottle. Once at the bottom, the salt moves out of the oil and into the water. This makes the oil again less dense than the water and the drops float back to the surface.

As more salt is added, the process is repeated several times. However, if you add too much salt, the process stops. This is because every time you add salt, it will eventually dissolve in the water and cause the density of the water to rise. Eventually the density of the salt water will become greater than the density of the salt and oil drops and the drops will no longer move from the surface to the bottom of the bottle.

Weird Science IN ACTION

The invention of the liquid motion lamp, commonly called the "lava lamp," is generally credited to a man named Edward Walker. One widespread story is that Walker came up with the basic design for the lamp in the 1950s while developing an egg timer. Another version says that Walker got the idea from a simpler liquid motion lamp he saw in an English pub. Either way, it was Walker who refined the idea into the lamps we see today. Walker died in August 2000, at the age of 82.

Commercial "lava lamps" use a slightly different process than you used in your experiment. The exact materials that are used are kept secret by the manufacturers, but they all use a difference in density to cause the globs to move.

In a real "lava lamp," the two substances have densities that are very similar. Another way to change density is by changing a material's temperature. Heating a substance causes its molecules to move faster and farther apart, which increases their volume slightly and this decreases their density. Motion lamps use a solid waxy compound and a liquid that have similar densities. When the lamp is off, the waxy compound is more dense than the liquid so it sits on the bottom of the lamp. But when the lamp is turned on and the waxy compound is heated, the waxy compound changes to a liquid and expands, giving it a lower density than the surrounding liquid. The warm blob begins to rise from the bottom of the container to the top of the liquid. But as the warm blob moves upward, it cools and becomes more dense than the liquid around it. It then returns to the bottom of the lamp and the process can start again.

2 WEIRD PLANTS

Way to Grow

All living organisms are divided into kingdoms. The animal kingdom and the plant kingdom are two examples. The plant kingdom includes all of the various kinds of trees, bushes, and grasses that we see every day, plus a few weird things that may surprise you.

Plants grow in many strange and wonderful ways. Most plants get their energy from the sun in a process called photosynthesis. In **photosynthesis,** a special substance in the plant called chlorophyll takes energy from the sun and uses it to make carbon dioxide and water into simple sugar molecules and oxygen. Animals eat the sugar molecules the plants make and breathe the oxygen they produce. Without plants, there wouldn't be any animals.

In addition to sunlight, water, and carbon dioxide, plants need other minerals to survive and need other animals—mostly insects—to help them reproduce. Many plants get the minerals they need from the soil they live in. But not all places where plants live have the minerals in the soil that they need, so some plants have developed interesting ways to get the nourishment they need. Still other plants have interesting ways to reproduce. So, to learn more about the world of weird plants, try the activities in this chapter.

PROJECT

The Eyes Have It

The fruits and vegetables we eat come from different kinds of plants and grow in different ways. Some fruits, like apples, grow on trees. Others, like blueberries, grow on bushes. Carrots and beets are roots that grow in the ground.

But a potato is different than many other vegetables. The potato doesn't grow on a tree or on a bush. It grows in the ground, but it's not a root crop. So how does it grow? Try this activity to learn more about how potatoes grow.

Materials

small potato
knife
paper bag

large clay pot
sandy soil
water
paper and pencil
adult helper

Procedure

1. Have an adult helper cut the potato into several pieces so that each piece contains at least two or three potato eyes. A potato's eyes are the indentation on the surface of the potato.

2. Lay the potato pieces in the sun for several days until the cut side of the potato dries out.

3. Place the potato piece in the paper bag and close it.

4. Set the bag in a dark place, such as a closet. Check it every other day until you begin to see buds (the first plant shoots) start to grow out of the potato's eyes.

5. Fill the clay pot half full of sandy soil.

6. Place the potato pieces in the soil, then cover them with the remaining soil. The potato should be covered with about 1 inch (2.5 cm) of soil.

7. Add a small amount of water to the soil so it is moist.

8. Place the pot in a sunny location.

9. Keep the soil moist by placing a small amount of water in the pot each day. Be careful not to add too much water.

10. For the next two to four weeks, observe how the potato grows and record what you see.

11. After one month, remove the plant from the soil and look at the roots. What do you notice?

Explanation

The potato plant will begin to grow, with shoots visible through the soil, in seven to ten days. The plant will continue to grow for the next few weeks, until it looks like a small bush. When you remove the potato plant from the soil after a month, you will notice long roots growing from the potato you planted with small round growths on the roots. These small round growths are called tubers and each will become a new potato.

Energy can be transformed from one form to another in many ways. One of the most common energy transfers that happens in nature is the conversion of light energy to chemical energy in plants. In photosynthesis, the energy from the sun causes chemical reactions that convert carbon dioxide and water into glucose and oxygen. The plant then uses the glucose to grow taller and stronger, or the glucose is stored in the form of starch for use later. **Starch** is a large molecule made up of many smaller sugar molecules linked together. Starch can be stored in various plant parts, such as in the roots or fruit.

In the case of the potato plant, that starch is stored in the potato tuber, the fleshy part of an underground stem of the potato plant. When the potato, or part of a potato, is placed in the soil, a main shoot begins to grow within a week or so. This main shoot will break through the soil and become the green plant that you saw growing above the soil. Its leaves undergo photosynthesis and the plant grows further. At about the time the main shoot breaks through the surface, rhizomes arise from underground nodes on the main shoot. A **rhizome** is a creeping stem that grows horizontally a few inches (cm) under the ground. The rhizomes grow horizontally underground for 5 to 12 inches (7.5 to 30 cm), then the tips thicken to form tubers. These tubers will develop into new potatoes.

PROJECT 2

Insect Eaters

Legend has it that the first Venus flytrap plant came to North Carolina from outer space aboard meteors. That's not really true, of course, but they are strange plants. The Venus flytrap gets its nourishment from eating insects instead of from photosynthesis. But the Venus flytrap is only one of several carnivorous plants. A **carnivorous** plant is one that needs the flesh of animals (in this case, small ones, like insects) in order to live.

But how can carnivorous plants eat insects? They don't have teeth or a stomach. To learn how they do it, try this activity.

Materials

4 small dishes
masking tape
felt-tip pen
iodine
eyedropper
soda crackers
timing device

Procedure

1. Place the dishes on the table. Use the tape and felt-tip pen to make labels for each dish. The labels should be: unchewed, 30 seconds, 5 minutes, and 10 minutes.

2. Place one soda cracker in the unchewed dish. Place a drop of iodine on the cracker. What happens?

3. Chew another cracker for 15 seconds, making sure that it becomes well moistened.

4. Place a third of the chewed cracker in each of the remaining dishes. Put a drop of iodine on the cracker in the 30-seconds dish. What happens?

5. Wait five minutes. Place a drop of iodine on the cracker in the 5-minutes dish. What happens?

6. Wait another five minutes then place a drop of iodine on the cracker in the 10-minutes dish. What happens?

Explanation

Iodine is a chemical that will turn dark blue or black when it reacts with starch. When iodine is placed on the unchewed cracker, the cracker will react by turning dark blue, indicating that starch is present. However, the chewed crackers will not turn dark blue when iodine is added. When iodine touches the cracker that was chewed and sat for 10 minutes it will stay its natural brown color. The starch is no longer present. When iodine touches the cracker that was chewed and sat for 5 minutes it will have a slightly blue/brown color. When it touches the cracker that was chewed before for 30 seconds it will have a darker blue/brown color. The longer you wait before putting the iodine on the chewed cracker, the less starch is there.

Starch is a large molecule made of many smaller sugar molecules. When you put food in your mouth and chew, saliva is added to the food. **Saliva** is an enzyme. An **enzyme** is a special chemical that makes chemical reactions happen faster. Saliva's main purpose is to break down long starch molecules into their component parts, the smaller sugar molecules. These smaller sugar molecules are later absorbed by the body in the intestines where they are used by cells for energy.

While carnivorous plants don't have teeth to chew up their food, they do have digestive juices, similar to the saliva you used in this activity. Their digestive juices are used to digest the insects they catch, the same way as the saliva helped to digest the cracker.

With the Venus flytrap, insects are attracted to the sweet-smelling nectar released between two open flaps that look similar to leaves. When an insect investigates the smell, it touches several small hairs on the flaps. When the hairs are touched two or three times, the flaps quickly close, trapping the insect between them. The Venus flytrap then releases its enzymes and the inside of the insect is dissolved and absorbed to feed the plant. After two or three days, the Venus flytrap opens and the outer skeleton of the insect is washed out by the rain and the plant is ready to lure another insect.

Weird Science IN ACTION

The pitcher plant, of the Sarracenia family of plants, is a carnivorous plant that lives in the slimiest bogs and marshes. **Botanists,** scientists who study plants, think that these plants developed the ability to eat bugs because the soil in the bogs and marshes didn't have enough nutrients to keep the plants alive. Each of the leaves of the pitcher plant is shaped like a pitcher or jug, with a slippery rim lined with stiff hairs that point downward into the hollowed leaves. The inside of the plant also has honey glands to attract insects. The downward pointing hairs and inviting aroma urge the insect to travel to the bottom of the pitcher. Once there, the insect finds that the plant's surface is also covered with a sticky substance and they can't escape the combination of sticky chemicals and stiff hairs. The insect dies and the plant then produces digestive juices to turn the bug into a nourishing soup the plant absorbs and uses to live.

So, how hungry is an insect-eating pitcher plant? In one study, a single plant, 2-feet (.6 m) tall, once ate seventy-three cockroaches during a two-week test period. If you do get one of these plants as a gift, make sure you feed it regularly or you may wind up being its next meal!

Spore Losers

You know that many plants reproduce from seeds. But not all plants reproduce this way. Some plants, called funguses (or fungi), use spores. **Spores** are very small reproductive cells that are dispersed by air. These spores have the ability to germinate into new plants. To learn more about fungus spores and see what they look like, try this activity.

Materials

large portobello mushroom (available from a grocery store)
dark colored paper (black or dark blue)
large bowl
spray fixative (available from an art supply store)
adult helper

Caution: This activity should not be done by anyone who is allergic to airborne particles or fungi. Your adult helper may know if you are allergic to these things.

Procedure

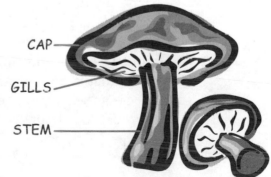

CAP
GILLS
STEM

1. Look at the mushroom. The top of the mushroom is called the cap. What do you notice about the gills on the underside of the mushroom cap?

2. Have your adult helper break off the stem of the mushroom leaving only the cap.

3. Lay the paper on the table in front of you.

4. Place the mushroom cap on the paper so that the gills are facing downward. Gently press the cap down onto the paper to slightly flatten it.

5. Invert the bowl over the mushroom so that the mushroom is completely covered.

6. Do not touch the mushroom, paper, or bowl for the next 24 hours.

7. After 24 hours, remove the bowl.

8. Next, very carefully remove the mushroom cap off the paper and throw it out. Do not touch the design on the paper. What does it look like?

More Fun Stuff to Do

You can preserve your mushroom design by sticking it in place with a spray fixative (available from an art supply store). Carefully, carry the paper outside. If it's windy, wait until a nonwindy day or the design will get blown away. Hold the can of fixative about 18 inches (45 cm) from the design that is on the paper and cover the design with spray. Let the fixative spray dry for about 15 minutes.

Explanation

After you remove the bowl and mushroom cap, you will notice a pattern of small specks. These specks look like a drawing of a wheel with a lot of spokes running out from a central point. If you spray the design with a fixative, you will be able to preserve the pattern.

The portobello mushroom is a fungus that has gills to hold its spores. When the mushroom is under the bowl, it is in the dark. This long dark period causes the mushroom to release spores from its gills. These spores fall onto the paper making the pattern you see.

Weird Science IN ACTION

While some mushrooms can be eaten and are very tasty, others are very poisonous. There is a mushroom called the death cap that can kill you if you eat it. Never eat any mushrooms that you find growing in the wild. Unless you really know what you're looking for, good mushrooms and bad mushrooms can look a lot alike.

PROJECT 4

"Corpse Flower"

Humans and other mammals rely greatly on their sense of sight to keep them safe and to find their way in the world. Other animals use different senses to do the same thing. Insects use their sense of smell to help them find their food. Some plants produce flowers that have a sweet fragrance to attract insects to them so the insects will pollinate them. But some plants, like the *Rafflesia arnoldi,* use an awful smell to attract insects. The *Rafflesia arnoldi* is the largest flower in the world. It weights 15 pounds (7kg) and grows only on the Sumatra Island of Indonesia. Its petals grow to 1.6 feet (.5m) long and 1 inch (2.5 cm) thick. But even as large and amazing as it looks, it's the smell of the *Rafflesia arnoldi* that is really weird. Another name for it is the "corpse flower" because is smells so bad. To see how smell can be used to guide insects, try this activity. Could you use your nose to find your way to a plant to help pollinate it?

Materials

blindfold
something smelly (e.g., perfume, vanilla extract,
    or crushed garlic)
cotton balls
small paper cup
paper towel
helper

*Note: Ask permission before moving the furniture to
perform this project.*

Procedure

1. For this experiment, you will need a large open space. Have your helper help you to push the furniture against the walls in a large room.

2. Soak several cotton balls in the smelly substance. Place the cotton balls in the paper cup.

3. Get your helper to act as the "insect" and try to make it from "home" (one side of the room) to the "flower" (the other side of the room where the smell cup is located) using only his or her sense of smell.

4. Blindfold your helper. Have him or her smell the cup with the cotton balls.

5. Have your helper get on hands and knees at the "home" side of the room.

6. Put the smell cup on the floor on the opposite side of the room. This will represent the flower your "insect" wants to find.

7. Have your helper crawl to the "flower" by using only the sense of smell.

8. If your helper has trouble finding the flower, place one of the cotton balls on a paper towel on the floor one or two yards (meters) away to help guide the "insect."

More Fun Stuff to Do

Repeat the activity using different smell cups each containing a different smelly substance. Which smell was easiest to find? Which smell was the most difficult?

Explanation

You and your helper should be able to find the cup after a little time. While our sense of smell is not as good as that of some insects, it is still remarkable.

It's very important that a plant can attract insects. As an insect is attracted to a plant's flower, pollen, the male part of the plant's reproductive system, gets stuck to the insect. When the insect then travels to another flower, the pollen drops off onto the female parts of the other plant, leading to reproduction and more plants.

Why does it help *Rafflesia arnoldi* to smell bad? Well, some insects, like flies, prefer bad smells over good smells because that's what they like to eat. That's why you see flies around rotting food and garbage. So, if you need flies to help you pollinate, you have to smell horrible. That's exactly what the *Rafflesia arnoldi* does!

Weird Science IN ACTION

The *Rafflesia arnoldi* plant is named after the two men who first discovered it. Sir Stamford Raffles discovered the plant with his friend, Dr. Joseph Arnold during their travels in Sumatra in 1818 and named it using their last names. Raffles later founded the British colony of Singapore in 1819. *Rafflesia arnoldi* doesn't grow outside its native Sumatra, but you may be lucky enough to see (and smell) another "corpse flower," the Titan Arum. These flowers are grown in a few botanic gardens in the United States, but they only bloom once every few years.

Epiphytes and Stranglers

All animals need oxygen in order to live, but not all animals get their oxygen from the air. Some animals, such as fish, get their oxygen from the water they live in. Similarly, all plants need water in order to live, but not all plants get their water from the soil through their roots. Some strange plants can get all the water they need as well as other nutrients, from the air. One kind of plant that lives this way is called epiphytes. These plants grow above the ground surface, using other plants or objects for support. They aren't rooted in the soil and aren't parasitic (they don't directly feed off of the plants they live on). So how do they get water? Try this activity to learn one way these plants get water from the air.

Materials

pot
water
stove
lid for the pot
oven mitt
adult helper

Procedure

1. Fill the pot half full of water.

2. Have your adult helper place the pot on the stove and turn the burner on.

3. Heat the water until it begins to boil, then turn off the burner.

4. Have your adult helper use the oven mitt to hold the lid for the pot at a slight angle above the water in the pot.

5. What happens on the bottom surface of the lid?

More Fun Stuff to Do

Go to a plant store and look at examples of epiphytes, such as bromeliads. Ask the owner how the plants get water.

Explanation

When the pot lid is placed above the hot water, drops of water will begin to form on it. After a few minutes the drops will begin to roll down the lid to the lower edge.

This activity shows how condensation works. When water is heated, whether by the burner on the stove, or by the heat of the sun, it changes state and becomes water vapor, the gas form of water. The water vapor rises and strikes the surface of the pot lid. Because the pot lid is cooler than the water vapor, the vapor will condense back into a liquid state, forming drops of water on the lid. As the drops grow larger, they roll down the lid toward its lower surface, pulled by the force of gravity.

This activity shows one way that epiphytes can get water. Most epiphytes are found in tropical rainforests where there is high humidity. **Humidity** is the amount of water that is in the air. Epiphytes use dew as their major source of water. During the day when the air is warm, water will stay in the air as water vapor. But at night, the air and plants begin to cool down. When this happens, the water vapor in the air will come in contact with the cooler plants and begin to condense to form liquid water. This water can be collected and taken in by the epiphytes.

If you go to a plant store and look at a bromeliad plant you will notice that they have a tightly rolled leaf structure that forms a funnel. As dew forms on the leaves, or as rain hits them, the water rolls down the leaf funnel and is stored at the bottom of the plant. Along with the water come plant debris and dust that supply nutrients that the plant also needs to live.

Another weird epiphyte is the strangler fig. The strangler fig begins life living on large canopy trees. **Canopy trees** are those that grow the highest in a forest, getting the most sunlight. The strangler fig will grow down and eventually outlive the host tree. The plant is know as a strangler because its root system will grow around the trunk of its host tree, forming an interlacing network that makes it look as if the plant is strangling the tree.

In addition to bromeliads and strangler figs, over half of the 20,000 species of orchids are epiphytes.

PROJECT 6

Cacti

As you saw in the last activity, plants can adapt to unusual conditions. In areas where it's very hot and dry, plants take on weird shapes to ensure they survive the harsh climate. One kind of plant that lives under these conditions are the cacti (plural for cactus). Cacti have a very shallow root system so that they can collect water near the surface, and their leaves have become sharp spines. How does this weird leaf structure help the cacti? Try this activity to find out.

Materials

glass baking pan
drinking glass
measuring cup
water

Procedure

1. Place the baking pan and the drinking glass on the table.

2. Measure ½ cup (125 ml) of water and pour it into the glass baking pan.

3. Pour ½ cup (125 ml) of water into the drinking glass.

4. Put the baking pan and the drinking glass in a place where the sun will directly hit each and where you can leave them for several days.

5. After several days, pour the water from the baking pan into the measuring cup and record how much there is. Empty the measuring cup and pour in the water from the drinking glass. How much of the original water was left in each container?

More Fun Stuff to Do

Go to a garden store and look in the section where they sell cacti. How many different kinds of cacti do you see? You will notice many different kinds of cacti that have spines. How many different kinds of spines can you find on them?

Explanation

After several days, more water will be left in the drinking glass than in the glass baking pan. When the sunlight strikes the water on the glass baking pan or the drinking glass, the water will begin to heat up. The water molecules near the surface will begin to change state from liquid to gas through the process of evaporation. **Evaporation** is the change of state from liquid to gas. Since the water in the baking pan has more surface area exposed to the sunlight, the water will evaporate faster than the water in the drinking glass.

The cactus is a member of a group of plants called succulents. **Succulents** are plants that can store water in their leaves, stems, and roots during the wet or rainy seasons in order to survive extended periods without water. Cacti store water in their stems. When it rains and there is more water available, the stem swells as it fills with water. When the rain stops, the stem contracts as the cactus uses the water in order to survive. Some cacti even have ribs that fill in and contract like an accordion during the year!

The cacti also have sharp spines instead of flat leaves. Flat leaves are good at photosynthesis and cooling the plant off through water evaporation. But evaporation is not good in hot dry areas. Flat leaves act like the water in the glass baking pan. There is more surface area exposed to sunlight, which leads to faster evaporation and a quicker water loss for the plant. In the cacti, photosynthesis occurs in the stems that remain green. Cactus spines have other advantages. The spines keep the plant from being eaten by animals. Because cacti grow slowly, they cannot afford to lose any of their plant mass to **herbivores** (animals that eat plants). Another function of the spines is to slow down winds, which reduces evaporation. Finally, the spines provide a surface on which water can condense during the cool desert nights. Any water that might be in the air at night condenses on the cactus spines, then drips to the ground where the roots can absorb it.

There are some really weird cacti that grow in the desert. The cholla cacti has multiple thorny stems that look soft and inviting, like a teddy bear, but are really sharp and can get under your skin. The old man cactus has spines that look like bushy white hair. These spines help the plant reflect the hot desert sun.

Weird Science IN ACTION

Many people grow cacti in their homes and gardens, but it was the Aztecs, of ancient meso-America who were the first to raise a specific species of cacti. It's recorded that they grew the *Opuntia coccenilla* cactus, which acts as a host to the cochineal scale insects. The Aztecs used the cacti to raise the insects, then harvested the insects for their scales (the hard outer shell that protects the insect's body). The Aztecs then crushed the insect scales to produce dye—a rich purple from the female scales or a brilliant scarlet from the male scales—used in fabrics and cosmetics.

3 WEIRD ANIMALS

No Pets Allowed

There are many different types of creatures in the animal kingdom, from tiny insects to giant whales. Each kind of animal has characteristics that allow it to survive in its environment. For example, animals have different body covering depending on where they live. Fish have scales that let them move smoothly through the water. Amphibians have smooth skin that they can breathe through. Reptiles have hard scales to protect them from drying out in the sun. Birds have feathers that help them fly. And mammals have hair and fur to keep them warm.

But some animals have some really weird characteristics that help them live and survive. To learn more, try the activities in this chapter.

Electric Eel

PROJECT

Animals have many interesting ways to protect themselves. Some use camouflage to help them blend in with their environment. Others have sharp teeth and choose to fight. But the electric eel's defense is downright shocking. Try this activity to find out how these slippery creatures keep predators away.

Materials

½-by-2-inch (1-by-5-cm) copper metal strip

½-by-2-inch (1-by-5-cm) zinc metal strip
    (available from a hardware store)

nail

hammer

lemon

2 pieces insulated #22 gauge copper wire, 12 inches (30 cm) long or
    wires with alligator clips. (Wires with alligator clips, which make
    electrical activities easier, can be purchased at most electronics
    stores.)

pliers

0.2-volt light bulb and holder or an LED (light emitting diode)
    (available at most electronics stores)

adult helper

Procedure

1. If you're using insulated wires, have an adult helper first make a hole in one end of each metal strip using the hammer and nail and then use the pliers to strip 1 inch (3 cm) of insulation from the ends of the wires.

2. Insert the copper and zinc strips into the lemon, about ½ inch (1.25 cm) apart.

3. Connect one end of each wire or the alligator clips to each of the strips. Thread the bare ends of the insulated wire through the holes in the strips and wrap the wire back on itself. Connect the other ends of the wire or alligator clips to the wires on the light bulb or LED. What happens?

More Fun Stuff to Do

Try placing the strips farther apart or closer together and observe the results. Experiment with using other types of metal strips or by substituting other fruits or vegetables. What happens?

Explanation

The light bulb will begin to glow when connected to the two metal strips placed in the lemon.

The electrical measurement **volt** is named after Alessandro Volta, an Italian scientist born in the eighteenth century. Volta discovered that certain chemical reactions could produce an electric current, which is a continuous flow of electrons. In order for the electrons to flow, a source of energy is needed. In the batteries you created the source of the energy is the pair of metals. One metal has a tendency to lose electrons while the other has a tendency to gain electrons. When these two metals are put into a chemical solution, such as the acid found in a lemon or potato, electrons will move from one metal to the other.

When you use the wires to complete the circuit between the two metals, you are able to use the energy created by the flow of electrons. This movement of electrons through the wires can light up a bulb or LED or can run a small digital clock.

The electric eel can generate an electric charge in a way similar to what you did in this activity. They don't have zinc and copper strips, but special organs inside their bodies contain chemicals that can gain or lose electrons. The result is that electric eels are able to produce electricity for short periods of time.

Electric eels live mainly in the Amazon River valley, where the waters are filled with dirt particles and it's just about impossible to see anything underwater. When the electric eel generates electricity, it creates an electric field around it. An **electric field** is the electrically charged area surrounding something that is creating or transmitting electricity. If the electric field around an electric eel is disturbed by another animal or even a rock, the eel can tell. They use this as a way for them to see in the murky waters where they live. But they also use their electric power to stun other animals. They can deliver a shock of up to 500 volts. This is enough to knock over a human or even a full-grown horse. A normal household plug delivers 120 volts. Repeated shocks from an eel can even cause death.

Weird Science IN ACTION

An electric eel is actually not an eel, but is one of a group of electric fish that emit an electrical discharge. While the electric eel is the most well known of this group, there are also electric catfish and electric rays. But the electric eel gives off the most powerful electric shock of them all!

PROJECT 2 Mudskippers

We normally think of fish as living in the water and breathing through **gills,** special organs that let fish take oxygen out of the water. But there are some weird fish that can swim in the water, crawl across the ground, and even climb trees! One of these weird fish is called the mudskipper. Try this activity to learn more about mudskippers and how they move on land.

Materials

large room

Procedure

1. Lie down on the floor on your stomach at one end of the room.

2. Lift yourself up onto your elbows.

3. Move both of your elbows forward a few inches (cm).

4. Holding your elbows on the floor, pull the rest of your body forward a few inches.

5. Continue to move by sliding your elbows forward and pulling yourself along.

More Fun Stuff to Do

Have a mudskipper race with a friend. Start at the same place then race to the opposite site of the room using the mud-skipper crawl in the activity above. Who is the fastest mudskipper?

Explanation

By moving your elbows forward, then using your arms to pull the rest of your body forward, you will be able to slowly move across the floor.

The mudskipper is a fish that has adapted to life in the **intertidal zone,** an area between the land and water near the rivers and lagoons of eastern Africa, Asia, and Australia. Mudskippers have armlike pectoral fins (the fins near a front of a fish's chest) that have little "elbows." They move by pushing both of their pectoral fins forward at the same time, then leaning on those fins and pulling the rest of their bodies forward in a little hop. Scientists call this kind of movement "crutching" because it's similar to the movement of a person on crutches.

When they are underwater, mudskippers breathe through gills the way other fish do. However, unlike most other fish, mudskippers can also live out of water as well. Other fish die when kept out of the water because their gill filaments stick together and cannot absorb oxygen. Mudskippers have a neat (and weird) trick that helps them survive. They take in a large amount of water before they head onto the land and keep it in an enlarged gill chamber that they lock shut. This acts kind of like reverse scuba gear. While on the land, the mudskippers move the water across their gills to get oxygen. But mudskippers can also breathe air! They can absorb oxygen directly from the air through membranes at the back of their mouths and throats, or directly through their skin as long as it's moist. This is similar to the way that amphibians, such as frogs, get some of their oxygen.

PROJECT 3

Weird Ants

What animal do you know that will eat every other animal in its path and will raid other colonies for food? Sound like a weird monster? Actually it's an ant. Not the ordinary ant that you see around your house. It's the army ant. The army ant is unique. A single colony of army ants may contain more than 1,000,000 ants. A colony needs to eat 50,000 insects each day, so it has to continually migrate from place to place looking for something to eat! But how do the ants of one colony all stay together and not get lost? Try this activity to find out.

Materials

a trail of ants

Procedure

1. Find a trail of ants. Watch the ants for a while and observe the path they take.

2. Use your index finger to rub across a small spot in the path.

3. What do the ants do when they reach the place you have rubbed?

4. Continue to observe the ants. What happens?

Explanation

The ants start out following a similar path on the ground, moving in a straight line. When you rub the path, the ants will stop walking in a line and will begin to walk left and right as they look for a path to follow. Eventually, a few ants will find the place on the other side of the place you rubbed where the path begins again. They will then continue following the path.

Ants are part of a family of insects called formicidae. They get their name from the chemical formic acid, which they release when they walk. That's how ants can walk along a path following one another. The first ants leave a trail of formic acid, which all the rest of the ants follow. When you rubbed your finger across the path, you erased the formic acid trail and the ants didn't know where to go. They began to search left and right, looking for the formic acid trail. When they found it again, they resumed their journey.

Army ants use a similar chemical message to mark the trails they take, so that other ants in their colony know where to go. Army ants are carnivores, and can eat animals much larger than themselves, including tarantulas, lizards, birds, snakes, pigs, and even sometimes animals as large as horses. Usually larger animals can get away from the slower moving army ants, but occasionally they are caught off guard.

An ant colony consists of queens, workers, and soldiers. The queen ant lays eggs the whole day. The larger soldiers work to defend the colony, medium-size workers forage for food, and small workers tend the queen and the emerging baby ants. Because of the large number of ants in the colony, army ants migrate in order to find food. They will often march at night and stop to camp in the day-time. From their base camp, smaller parties of ants move out creating raid fronts as they look for food. If the path a raid group travels has a lot of food, the rest of the colony will follow their trail and the colony will move to a new location.

Because army ants kill almost all insects in their path, they are sometimes welcomed by villagers who live in parts of South America. The army ants provide a free natural pest-control service. Rather than fight the army ants, villagers will leave their homes as the army ants approach. They will return to their village later and find it totally insect-free!

Banana Slugs

PROJECT 4

Have you ever seen a banana walking? You have if you've encountered the weird banana slug. A slug is something like a naked snail, because it has no shell. Slugs and snails are both mollusks, and they both like damp, moist weather. You may have seen slugs in your garden. They are often small and dark colored. But banana slugs can grow as large as a banana—up to 10 inches (25 cm) long. They are found in moist forest floors along the Pacific Coast of North America, from California to Alaska. They get their name not only from their size, but also their color. Banana slugs are often bright yellow with black spots. Banana slugs can also be greenish, pale brown, or even almost white. Their colors can change slightly over time because of the plants they eat, which helps them blend in better with their surroundings. The slug moves on one large muscular foot. But how can anything move with only one foot? To learn more about how slugs move, try this activity.

Materials

glass jar with a lid (clean and dry)
nail
hammer
grass
slugs
spray bottle with water
adult helper

Procedure

1. Have your adult helper use the hammer and nail to make several small holes in the lid of the jar.

2. Place some grass in the bottom of the jar.

3. On a damp day, go outside into a garden or wooded area with your adult helper.

4. Look under rocks and leaves to find several slugs.

5. Once you have found several, place them in the jar and tightly place the lid back on.

6. Take the slugs home for observation. Look at a slug when it is moving along the side of the glass jar, so you can see it from underneath. What happens along its underside as it moves?

More Fun Stuff to Do

Remove the jar lid and touch the area right behind where a slug has traveled. What does it feel like? (Once you are done observing your slugs, return them to the garden or place where you found them. They are an important part of the local ecosystem.)

Explanation

As a slug moves along the glass surface, you will notice waves of motion along its underside. The area on the jar right behind where the slug moved will feel rather slimy.

Both banana slugs and the common slugs you find in your garden travel on one big foot, the part of their body that you looked at through the glass. The waves you saw were caused by the slug slowly moving parts of its foot forward one at a time. Once one part of the foot has moved forward, the next part gets a chance. We see that as a wave motion on the underside of the slug's foot.

The slippery stuff behind a slug when they move is called **mucus.**

A slug has special cells just behind its head to make the mucus, which it needs to move. The mucus makes the ground just below the slug into a slippery track that the slug can move on. The ground would be too rough for slugs to travel without the mucus. Sometimes, when you look in your garden in the morning, you will notice a silvery path of dried mucus that a snail or slug has left behind.

The second purpose of the mucus is to protect the slug from predators. Most animals and birds do not like the slimy texture that it gives the slug. Also, the slime contains an anesthetic that temporarily causes moist skin, like that inside the mouth, to go numb. Raccoons will eat slugs but will first roll them in dirt to get rid of the slime.

Weird Science IN ACTION

Every year in Elma, Washington, people gather to watch a competition to see who will become the "World's Fastest Slug." The slugs (usually banana slugs) race on a 24-inch (60-cm) track that is lined with salt, a chemical that slugs hate. Just in case you're wondering, the average garden snail moves at .005 mph (.008 km/hr), so the race takes a while to complete.

PROJECT 5

Dung Beetles

Decomposition is the natural process of decay. It is also a very important part of life. Imagine what would happen if everything that died did not decompose. Leaves from the trees would pile up year after year. Dead insects, animals, and birds would soon cover the ground. And the waste from living organisms would just stay where it fell. Fortunately there are creatures such as bacteria, slugs, and even birds like vultures that help nature recycle the nutrients in dead organisms.

One of the weirdest decomposers is the dung beetle. It likes to eat— you guessed it—dung, or animal poop. Most of the dung in the world is produced by what are called megaherbivores, like cows, horses, and elephants. A herbivore is an animal that eats plants. Mega means big. So megaherbivores are large plant-eating animals. Their digestive systems can digest only a part of the plants they eat, so their dung contains a lot of partially digested plants which still contain nutrients. That's where the dung beetles come in, which is a good thing because some megaherbivores, like elephants, have really big dung!

To learn more about what dung beetles do, try this activity to learn how materials can decompose.

Materials

clear, plastic 2-quart (2-liter) soda bottle (clean and dry)
scissors
cheesecloth
rubber band
tape
2 cups (500 ml) of sand
2 quarts (2 liters) of garden soil taken from an outdoor location
organic material such as leaves, twigs, grass, newspaper, and pine needles
inorganic material such as Styrofoam, plastic, and scraps of fabric or leather
paper and pencil
worms (optional)
water
stick
several sheets of newspaper
rubber gloves
adult helper

Procedure

1. Soak the bottle in hot water for about ½ hour to loosen the label, then peel off the label.

2. Have your adult helper cut the bottle into two pieces, cutting approximately ⅓ the way from the bottom.

3. Cover the mouth of the bottle with a piece of cheesecloth and secure it with the rubber band.

4. Turn the top section of the bottle upside down and place it in the bottom section as shown. Tape the two sections together.

5. Place the sand in the upside down container. Place 1 cup (250 ml) of garden soil on top of the sand.

6. Look at the organic and inorganic material that you have collected. Which items do you think will decompose quickly? Why? Which items do you think will take longer to decompose? Why? Record your predictions.

7. Add a small amount of organic and inorganic material to the container, then add another layer of soil. Continue to layer organic and inorganic materials and soil until you reach the top of the container. Add more material on top of the last layer of soil.

8. (Optional) Add worms to the container.

9. Pour water into the container until it drips through the cheesecloth.

10. Set the container where it will not be disturbed for a month. Water the container twice a week.

11. Observe the container every other day. Record your observations.

12. After a month, put on the rubber gloves and pour out the contents of the container onto the newspaper. Use the stick to move the soil around. Observe the condition of the organic and inorganic material. Were your predictions correct?

Caution: Always wear rubber gloves when examining the experiment. Throw out the project when you are finished. Be sure to wash your hands thoroughly when you are done.

Explanation

After several weeks, the organic material will begin to decompose and disappear and will be harder to find in the soil.

Decomposition is nature's way to recycle organic or living material. Organic material is broken down into nutrients that can be reused by plants as they grow. Some inorganic or nonliving material is broken down as well, but usually at a slower rate. Bacteria, fungi, worms, and other small organisms all help break down these materials.

Worms in particular help speed up the process of decomposition. They make extensive networks of tunnels that help air and water reach the roots of plants. The tunnels also provide air and water for other soil insects and small organisms that help with the process of decomposition. Worms also turn the soil by moving deep soil up to the surface and dragging plant materials underground.

One cup of soil may contain more than 5 billion living creatures. All of these creatures help decomposition, but getting rid of dung is the special job of the dung beetles. Dung beetles can be divided into three groups: rollers, tunnelers, and dwellers. Rollers are more common in tropical areas. When rollers find dung, they roll pieces of it into small- or medium-size balls, then roll these balls over the ground from the dung pile to their home burrows. A tunneler dung beetle will fly along until it finds a nice pile of dung, like a fresh cow pad. Usually in pairs, the beetles then dive in the dung pile and dig a tunnel beneath it. The female dung beetle will stay in the tunnel and sort out the dung that the male drags down from the surface. Dweller dung beetles make their home inside the dung. They lay their eggs there and when the larvae hatch, they happily eat their fill. By dragging dung below the soil's surface, dung beetle help recycle the nutrients in dung by returning it to the soil where plants can use it.

Weird Science IN ACTION

Roller dung beetles can stay inside their burrows and care for their eggs and young for up to three years. Some of these dung beetles are incredibly strong and can move balls of dung that are up to 50 times their weight! If humans were that strong, a 110-pound (50-kg) person could move a ball that weighed 5,500 pounds (2,500 kg)—almost 3 tons!

PROJECT Naked Mole Rats

In the Weird Ants activity you learned that ants leave a chemical trail to guide them as they move in a line from one place to another. Other animals use other senses. Humans mainly use sight and hearing; other animals use taste or smell. But some animals live mainly below the surface of the earth, with nothing to see and little to smell. How do they know what's around them?

The nearly blind naked mole rats spend most of their lives burrowing through the ground. They are nearly hairless, usually about 3 inches (7.5 cm) long, and weigh less than 2 ounces (30 g). So how do they get around? Try this activity to find out.

Materials

larger room
helper
cloth for a blindfold
kitchen chairs

Note: Ask permission before moving the furniture to perform this project.

Procedure

1. For this experiment, you will need a large open space. Have your helper help you push the furniture against the walls in a large room.

2. Sit on one side of the room.

3. Cover your eyes with the blindfold and tie it behind your head so it stays in place.

4. Have your helper put several chairs or other obstacles in the middle of the room.

5. Crawl on your hands and knees from one side of the room to the other. How can you know where to go without using your eyes?

More Fun Stuff to Do

Have your helper make an obstacle course for you to travel through as you go from one side of the room to the other. Have some objects you need to go around and others you need to go under. Does this make your trip more difficult?

Explanation

You should be able to move from one side of the room to the other without using your eyes. You learn, after bumping into a few things, to use your sense of touch to get around. With more obstacles in your path, traveling will be more difficult, but still possible.

Humans and many other animals use their sense of sight to figure out where to go. But naked mole rats have adapted to living underground where there is no light to see by. Mole rats are found in Africa, in eastern Ethiopia, central Somalia, and Kenya. They walk on all four feet, similar to the way you crawled across the floor. They can move forward and backward quickly and can even somersault in the tunnels. They communicate with honks and squeaks, and they use their noses and whiskers to feel around the tunnels. They also may communicate over long distances by creating patterns of vibrations that travel through the ground.

Because they live mainly in hard soils, they mostly dig after a rain, when the soil is easier to move. They stay deep underground during the day to avoid the hot temperatures near the surface. They live in well-organized colonies of about 20 to 30 mole rats. Mole rats are unique among vertebrates in that, as in insect colonies, the colony members include workers, gatherers, and one dominant queen mole rat, who leads the colony and has all the babies. They have sharp teeth that they use to chisel the earth. When they dig a new burrow, one mole rat will literally eat through the dirt and create a pile of soil behind him. Other mole rats will use their legs to kick the soil backward through the tunnel, passing the dirt from mole rat to mole rat until it reaches the surface. The mole rat eats roots and tubers found below the surface of the soil.

PROJECT

Gone Batty

Even among all the other weird animals, bats really stand out. They are the only mammals that can fly and they spend most of their lives hanging upside down in dark caves. They are most active at night, leading to all sorts of myths and stories. Bats are well known for sucking blood, but there are actually only a few species that do that.

Since bats fly mainly at dusk, night, and dawn, they need more than just their eyesight to find their food, which for many bats means flying insects. Bats use a system of echolocation to help them locate objects. To learn about echolocation, try this activity.

Materials

rooms in your home

Procedure

1. Stand facing a wall on one side of a room.

2. Cup your hands behind your ears so that your palms face forward and say "hello" several times. How does it sound to you?

3. Walk to an open doorway and again say "hello" several times. How does your voice sound this time?

4. Try moving close to other objects, such as a chair or a lamp, to see how your voice sounds when you say "hello" in the direction of the object.

5. Move different distances from a wall, close your eyes, and then say "hello." Can you tell how far you are from the wall by simply listening to your voice?

More Fun Stuff to Do

Close your eyes and try to walk around the room as you speak. Can you find your way from the middle of the room to the door by simply listening to the changes in your voice as you speak?

Explanation

You will notice that the sound of your voice will change as you stand in front of different objects. Your voice will seem louder when you are right in front of a wall and quieter when you are near the open door.

When you speak, the movement of your vocal cords creates sound waves. When these sound waves hit a solid object, the waves reflect, or bounce off, the object. Some of these waves are reflected back toward your ears and you hear them, making the sound seem louder. Cupping your hands behind your ears helps you collect more sound waves, the way a bat's large ears do. When you stand near the open doorway the sound waves aren't reflected, so your voice doesn't sound as loud. With practice, you will be able to tell how far away an object is by simply listening to the sound of your voice as it reflects off the object and returns to your ear. This is how echolocation works.

Bats use their keen sense of hearing to find their way in the dark. Bats emit high pitched sounds from their mouths and noses. Some of the sounds are at a frequency beyond the human hearing range, but they behave in the same way as the sounds that come out of your mouth. They can bounce off solid objects and return to the bats' ears. The bats listen to the reflected sounds and their brains translate the sounds into information about where objects are, how big they are, and in what direction they are moving. For example, a bat can tell if a flying insect is to the right or left of it by comparing the sounds that reach its right and left ears.

The most common bat is the brown bat, which can eat as many as 1,200 mosquitoes per hour. A large colony of Mexican free-tail bats lives in Bracken Cave, Texas. More than 20 million bats live in this cave, and when they come out at night for dinner, they eat roughly 200 tons of insects.

Weird Science IN ACTION

The weirdest of all bats may be the vampire bats. Vampires are a mixture of fact and fiction. They do indeed drink blood, but they aren't Dracula! They merely prick an animal and lap up the blood that flows out. A special chemical in vampire bat saliva keeps the blood from clotting. Vampire bats need only about 2 tablespoons (30 ml) of blood per day to survive, and they never actually consume enough blood to kill the animals they feed on. However, vampire bats can be dangerous because they sometimes carry rabies. Vampire bats are only found in Central and South America.

4 WEIRD MICROBES

The Good, the Bad, the Smelly

In previous chapters you learned about some weird plants and animals, two of the kingdoms that we divide all living organisms into. But there are other kingdoms as well. One is known as the monera kingdom and the creatures in it, also known as microbes or micro-organisms, are the oldest and most abundant living organisms known.

The monera kingdom includes all bacteria and several other forms of one-celled organisms. A simple one-celled organism known as blue-green algae, which is a member of this kingdom, appears in the fossil record that dates back 3.5 billion years!

Most bacteria display one of three basic shapes: spherical (called cocci), rod-shaped (called bacilli), and spiral (called spirilla). Bacteria do many good things for us, like the ones that live in your intestines and form vitamin B and vitamin K from the food you eat. But they can also make you sick, like the streptococcus bacteria (it has a spherical shape as its name says) that can give you a nasty sore throat.

If you want to learn more about some of the weird microbes that share our world with us, try the following activities.

PROJECT

Smelly Feet

We carry many organisms on our bodies that are too small to see. These tiny microbes perform lots of tasks for us. They also can leave some unwanted side effects, like smelly feet and intestinal gas. Try this activity to discover the microbes that make feet smell.

Materials

adult helper
½ cup (125 ml) water
4 packages of unflavored gelatin
cooking pan
1-quart (1-liter) jar with lid
tennis shoes
cotton swab
rubber gloves
Note: This procedure requires adult help.

Procedure

1. Have your adult helper prepare the gelatin by boiling the water in the pan and dissolving the gelatin in the boiling water.

2. Allow the gelatin to cool until it is cool enough to handle but not solid (about 5 minutes).

3. When the gelatin has cooled, pour it into the jar.

4. Hold the jar over a trash can and tip it horizontally. Let the extra gelatin pour out until only enough gelatin remains in the jar to cover its side.

5. Set the jar on its side and leave it undisturbed for four hours until the gelatin hardens.

6. Put your tennis shoes on without socks and go play outside for a while.

7. When you come back inside, remove your shoes. Take the cotton swab and rub it between all your toes.

8. Reach into the jar and carefully brush the gelatin with the cotton tip. Make a wavy line in the gelatin as shown.

9. Place the lid on the jar and put the jar in a warm, dark location. Leave it there for four days.

10. Wash your hands and feet.

11. After the four days, observe the gelatin in the jar. What do you see? *Caution: Do not touch the gelatin because many microbes can cause disease!* Don't keep the jar longer than four days to keep the microbes from multiplying too much. When you are done with the experiment, put on rubber gloves, fill the jar with hot water, let it soak for five minutes and then wash the jar. The gelatin will dissolve and can be washed down the sink. Be sure to wash your hands when you are finished, and dispose of the jar.

Explanation

After a few days you will begin to see grooves in the gelatin. These are places where the gelatin has been eaten by microbes.

Like other parts of your body, feet sweat. In addition, dead skin cells fall off of them. The inside of your shoes is dark, warm, and damp from sweat. This is a perfect environment for microbes to grow, since they like warm, dark, damp places. The most common bacteria that cause your feet to smell are corynebacteria and micrococci.

Your jar has a similar environment. The gelatin provides the microbes with food and a nice place to live, so they eat and reproduce. The waste the microbes produce is what gives sweaty tennis shoes and your feet that terrific smell.

Microbes can be found just about everywhere on and around your body, even on your skin and eye lashes.

Weird Science IN ACTION

Believe it or not, each of your feet has over 20,000 sweat glands. Through these sweat glands, you produce about a half a cup of sweat each day, which creates the perfect microbe environment.

To keep these bacteria from making your feet too smelly, make sure to wear clean socks with your sneakers. You can also use powder on your feet to keep them dry.

PROJECT 2 Early Risers

If you've ever helped make bread, did you know that you were putting a living thing in the dough? To find out about how microbes help make yummy breads and other baked goods, try this activity.

Materials

1 package of dry yeast
measuring spoons
mixing bowl
measuring cup

warm water
mixing spoon
resealable plastic bag
sugar

Procedure

1. Place one tablespoon (15 ml) of dry yeast in a mixing bowl.

2. Add one cup of warm (not hot) water to the yeast and use the spoon to mix the two ingredients together.

3. Pour about ¼ cup of the mixture into the plastic bag.

4. Add one tablespoon (15 ml) of sugar the bag.

5. Close the bag so that all the air in the bag is removed, then reseal the opening.

6. Place the plastic bag in a warm location, such as a sunny windowsill or on top of a warm oven.

7. Leave the bag alone for about 15 minutes. What do you notice about the bag when you return?

8. Open the bag and smell the contents. What does it smell like?

More Fun Stuff to Do

Try the experiment again, but this time add different substances to the yeast mixture. Try adding flour, syrup, or grape juice in place of the sugar. What happens?

Explanation

The plastic bag of yeast will begin to fill with gas after about 15 minutes. When you sniff inside the bag, you will smell a distinctive smell. When you add flour, syrup or grape juice to the yeast mixture, you will get similar results.

Yeast is a single-celled fungus. When you add the yeast to warm water, it begins to grow. As it grows, it needs food. Sugar supplies food to the yeast cells. What the yeast cells do with sugar is called **fermentation,** the breaking down of complex molecules without the use of oxygen. In this case, yeast cells turn sugar into carbon dioxide gas and alcohol. As the carbon dioxide gas is released, it causes the plastic bag to inflate. When you opened the plastic bag, you could also smell the alcohol that the yeast forms during fermentation. The yeast can use many things as food during the fermentation process, including sugar, flour, syrup, or grape juice.

Bakers use yeast in baking bread because of the gas that is released during fermentation. When yeast is added to flour and water, the yeast begins to turn some of the flour first into sugar and then into carbon dioxide and alcohol. The carbon dioxide gas gets trapped in the sticky bread dough, which causes the bread to rise. The little holes you see in bread were created by the carbon dioxide gas bubbles. The alcohol that forms evaporates during the baking process and the yeast cells are destroyed by the heat. What you have in the end is a loaf of fresh-baked bread!

Weird Science IN ACTION

Yeast is also used to make wine. Yeast is added to grape juice and causes fermentation creating carbon dioxide gas and alcohol. In making the wine, the carbon dioxide gas is usually released, leaving the alcohol mixed in the grape juice.

PROJECT 3

Galdieria Sulphuraria

Plants and animals can live in all sorts of different environments. Polar bears, for example, can live in the very cold Arctic temperatures and orchids can live in very hot, humid tropical regions. Some bacteria can live in even more harsh environments, but the prize for extreme survival goes to the *Galdieria sulphuraria,* a red algae that prefers to live in highly acidic, sulphur hot springs.

To learn more about one of the conditions needed for this weird organism to live, try this activity about acids.

Materials

red cabbage
2 quarts (2 liters) of tap water
2-quart pot
strainer
plastic bowl
5 small jars
marking pen
1 teaspoon (5 ml) lemon juice
1 teaspoon (5 ml) vinegar
1 teaspoon (5 ml) bottled water
1 teaspoon (5 ml) baking soda
1 teaspoon (5 ml) ammonia
adult helper

Procedure

1. Tear two red cabbage leaves into small pieces. Ask your adult helper to boil them for 5 minutes in the 2 quarts (2 liters) of water.

2. Hold the strainer over the plastic bowl and have your helper pour the mixture through the strainer. Strain off the leaves and throw them away. Allow the colored liquid to cool in the plastic bowl.

3. Set up five small jars and pour ½ cup (125 ml) of the cooled cabbage water into each. Number the jars 1 through 5 with the marking pen.

4. Add the lemon juice to jar #1, the vinegar to jar #2, the bottled water to jar #3, the baking soda to jar #4, and the ammonia to jar #5. *Caution: Be careful not to spill ammonia on your hands.*

5. Observe the color that each chemical turns the cabbage water and record the color on a chart similar to the one on the next page.

Jar-Chemical	Acid/Base	Color
1—lemon juice	acid	
2—vinegar	slightly acid	
3—bottled water	neutral	
4—baking soda	slightly base	
5—ammonia	base	

6. Collect several different water samples and test them with a small amount of cabbage juice to determine how acid each sample is. For example, test your tap water, some rain water, or the water in a nearby pond. How acidic is the water that is used to water the plants in your area?

More Fun Stuff to Do

Try adding several tablespoons of lemon juice to the water that you use to water a small plant. How does an increase in the acidity of the water affect the plant's growth?

Explanation

In the first part of this activity you used cabbage water as a chemical indicator. When a chemical indicator is mixed with an acid or a base, a chemical reaction occurs. The exact reason why an indicator changes color when mixed with an acid or base has been studied for many years. It appears that the acid or base changes the structure of the atoms of the indicator by changing the way its electrons fit around the nucleus of its atoms. This causes the change in the color of the indicator.

Cabbage water will change color depending on the type of solution that is added. Listed next are the expected results.

Jar-Chemical	Acid/Base	Color
1 - lemon juice	acid	red
2 - vinegar	slightly acid	pink
3 - bottled water	neutral	dark purple
4 - baking soda	slightly base	light green
5 - ammonia	base	green

The cabbage water will also change color to indicate the amount of acid or base of the water samples you tested. Most water is near neutral, but pollution in the air can cause rain water to be more acidic (called "acid rain"). If acidic water is added to a plant, it will usually begin to die.

Most land plants need water and soil conditions where the water is near neutral. Some plants can adapt to slight changes in the acidity of the soil, but most plants will die with high acidity.

But the single-celled red algae called *Galdieria sulphuraria* prefers very acidic conditions, even more acidic than pure lemon juice! They also can survive temperatures above 133°F (56°C). They have been found in volcanic areas in Italy, Iceland, and the Azore Islands off the coast of Spain. When there is not enough light for photosynthesis, some *Galdieria sulphuraria* will live by absorbing nutrients from others cells as they die.

5 WEIRD WEATHER

Ball Lightning, Rogue Waves, and Twisting Tornadoes

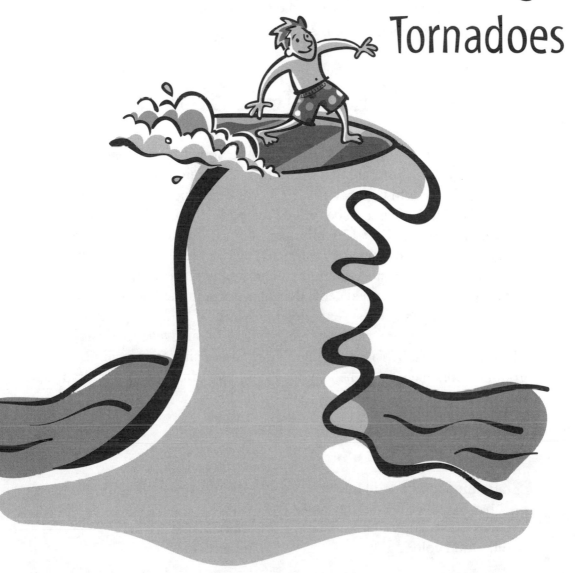

Weather is the local condition of the atmosphere in and near a particular area. It includes the usual sunshine, rain, snow, and wind, but it can also include some stuff that's pretty weird, like giant waves, extreme winds, and lightning shaped like balls. One thing is common to all weather: it needs air in order to form. The moon for example, doesn't have weather because it doesn't have an atmosphere. Earth's atmosphere extends for about 300 miles (500 km) up from the surface, held in place by gravity. Our changing weather is produced by changes in temperature, humidity (amount of moisture), and movement of air in the atmosphere.

Different combinations of wind, water, and temperature cause many of the different phenomena we see in the skies. To learn more about weird weather, try the activities in this section.

PROJECT

The Perfect Storm

Waves in the ocean are formed by a combination of winds, tides, and currents. Sometimes, when conditions are just right, the waves can grow very large. In October 1991, a storm developed off the New England coast that came to be called "the perfect storm." This rare combination of winds of 120 miles per hour (192 km/hr) and weather created ocean waves that were estimated at 100 feet (30 m) tall! Such weirdly large waves are sometimes called rogue waves. The largest rogue waves ever recorded came during a storm in the Pacific Ocean. A low-pressure weather system blowing winds of 80 miles per hour (130 km/hr) for over a week straight resulted in one wave that was 112 feet (34 m) tall. The wave hit a Navy tanker ship from behind, giving sailors the ride of their lives as the wave lifted the ship up into the air and set it down again.

Try this activity to find out how waves move.

Materials

tall, thin jar with a lid (clean and dry)—an olive jar will work,
  but the taller the jar, the better
water   spoon
blue food coloring   mineral oil

Procedure

1. Fill the jar half full with water.

2. Add several drops of food coloring to the water and stir with the spoon.

3. Fill the jar to the very top with mineral oil.

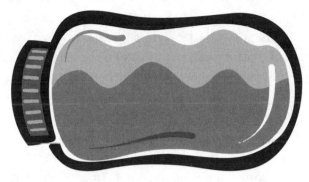

4. Place the lid on the jar and twist on tightly.

5. Hold the jar horizontally in front of you. What do you notice about the water and oil?

6. Slowly lift one end of the jar then bring it back to the horizontal. What do the water and oil do this time? What does it look like?

More Fun Stuff to Do

Try moving one end of the jar up and down more quickly. What happens inside the jar this time? What do you have to do to make very large waves?

Explanation

When you first look at the water and oil, the blue water is below the clear mineral oil. When you tip one end of the jar and bring it back again, it creates a wave of blue water inside the jar that moves slowly from one end of the jar to the other. By moving the jar rapidly you can make very large waves that crash about inside the jar.

A wave is a way to transfer energy from one place to another. The highest point of a wave is called the **crest** and the lowest point is called the **trough**. The distance between wave crests is the **wavelength** of the wave and the distance from the middle of a wave to its crest is the wave's **amplitude**. In this activity, you created a **transverse wave,** a wave that moves perpendicular to its source. An ocean wave is also a transverse wave.

The main wave-building force on the ocean is wind, although tides and currents can affect ocean waves as well. The force of the wind against the ocean's surface causes areas of the ocean to move upward. As the water moves upward, it gains potential energy. These places where water moves upward are called swells. Later, these swells will form the crest of a wave. If the wind blows on the surface of the water for a longer period of time, the waves will continue to move upward, gaining even more potential energy. If one wave absorbs enough wind energy to grow much larger than all the waves around it, it's called a rogue wave and can do a lot of damage to anything in its path. Little is known about why these rogue waves form, as they have also been seen unexpectedly in calm weather and quiet seas.

Once the swells have formed, they begin to move out like ripples around a pebble dropped in a pond. But while the swell (and its energy) moves out, the water molecules themselves only move up and down. As these swells enter shallow coastal waters, they begin to change. When the water depth is about one half the wavelength, the incoming swell begins to get resistance from the ocean floor. Because of this resistance, the swell slows down and the distance between crests decreases. As this happens, the back of the wave begins to catch the front of the wave, the wave begins to grow taller, and the front of the wave becomes steeper. The crest of the wave then begins to fall forward in what is called a **break.** But the wave still has all its energy. That energy is given up as the wave crashes into the beach.

Weird Science IN ACTION

Another way that very large waves can be created is by an earthquake. These waves are called tsunamis and are caused by the sudden vertical displacement of the ocean floor. (They are formed in a way similar to what you created by moving your glass jar up and down rapidly.) Usually an earthquake greater than 6.5 on the Richter Scale (a very strong earthquake) is necessary to create a tsunami. After the violent earthquake, a tsunami wave can be produced that is 600 miles (1000 km) long and can move at speeds faster than 500 miles per hour (800 km/hr). Tsunamis can travel thousands of miles across the ocean without losing very much energy. An earthquake in Chile in 1960 caused sixty-one deaths in Hilo, Hawaii, when the 100-foot (30 m) wave crested when it hit the island.

Ball Lightning

Any kind of lightning is pretty strange when you think about it. How can clouds create these huge bursts of electricity? But some kinds of lightning are even weirder than usual. Ball lightning for example, consists of bright, hovering spheres of light seen during some thunderstorms they have been reported as far back as the ancient Greeks. The glowing spheres can be as small as a tennis ball or as large as a beach ball. Ball lightning can even seem to go through solid walls.

No one knows for sure what causes ball lightning. While regular lightning is caused by an electrical discharge, one theory states that ball lightning is possibly a plasma state of matter. **Plasma** is a fourth state of matter (after solid, liquid, and gas) that is common in the universe, but very rare on Earth.

But two New Zealand scientists have another theory about ball lightning. And to understand their theory, you need to understand regular lightning and what causes it. Try this activity to find out more about lightning.

Materials

paper towel
1 teaspoon (5 ml) crispy rice cereal
balloon
wool sweater

Procedure

1. Place the paper towel on the table.

2. Put the cereal on the paper towel.

3. Blow up the balloon and knot the end.

4. Rub the balloon several times on the wool sweater.

5. Bring the balloon near the cereal. Observe what happens.

More Fun Stuff to Do

Put on your shoes and shuffle your feet across the carpet in your house for 15 seconds. Walk to the door then slowly bring your finger close to the doorknob. When your finger is about ¼ inch (.65 cm) from the knob, what happens?

Note: This activity works best on a cold winter day when the heat is on in your home.

Explanation

The cereal is attracted to the balloon. In the More Fun Stuff to Do, after shuffling your feet on the carpet, you will notice that there is a spark that jumps from your finger to the knob and you feel a small electric shock.

This activity works because of *static electricity,* which is electricity that does not flow. Static electricity builds up with friction, which is caused by two objects, like wool and a balloon, rubbing together. All objects are made of atoms, and every atom has an equal number of protons and electrons. Protons have a positive charge and electrons have a negative charge. When these charges are equal, an object is neutral or uncharged. Some objects, however, such as wool or hair, easily lose electrons. When you rubbed the balloon with the wool, some electrons moved from the wool to the balloon. The balloon then had a negative static charge.

The balloon can induce an electric charge in a neutral charged object. This is called charging by induction. When you bring the negatively charged balloon near the crispy cereal, the negatively charged balloon repels the electrons in each piece of cereal. The electrons move to the opposite side of the cereal. This gives the side of the cereal nearest the balloon a positive static charge (an induced charge) and it is attracted to the negatively charged balloon. The crispy rice is attracted to the balloon. Over a longer period of time, the electrons will transfer from the balloon to the cereal. Eventually, the balloon will become neutral and the cereal will fall back to the table.

When you shuffle your shoes against a carpet you again create friction and you pick up extra electrons from the carpet. Those electrons are actually stored on the surface of your body. When you bring your finger near the doorknob, these electrons will jump from your body to the knob, creating the spark you see.

Charging by induction and the spark that follows can also occur during thunderstorms. As clouds move across the sky, they pick up extra electrons from the air, similar to the way the balloon got electrons from the wool sweater and your body got them from the carpet. The negatively charged cloud then induces a positive charge on the surface of the earth. When the electrical charge between the clouds and the earth's surface is great enough, there is an electrical discharge as the electrons in the clouds move to the surface trying to make both electrically neutral. We see this discharge as a giant spark of lightning.

John Abrahamson and James Dinniss from Canterbury, New Zealand, think that ball lightning is actually burning particles of silicon. When ordinary lightning hits the ground, mineral grains in the soil can be converted into tiny particles of silicon, an element that is very abundant in the earth. These particles are very small—less than a millionth of a yard (meter) in size. The scientists think these particles link together to form chains that fold back on themselves to form light, fluffy balls that are carried upward by air currents. These silicon balls are very reactive and burn very slowly. As the particles burn, they release light. Abrahamson and Dinniss think that right after a normal lightning strike has finished, the air it has traveled through is free to erupt and burn the silicon balls that appear above the ground. We see this as ball lightning.

Weird Science IN ACTION

Benjamin Franklin was the first to demonstrate the negative charge in clouds in his famous kite-flying experiment. He also discovered that when lightning travels from a cloud to the earth, it moves to tall, pointed objects first. From this fact, he developed the first lightning rods. These rods were placed on houses and had electric wires that ran from the rods on the top of the house to the ground. When there was lightning in the area, the lightning would strike the lightning rods, rather than the house, and the electrical discharge would be harmlessly directed into the earth's surface.

Extreme Winds

 **PROJECT 3**

Wind can blow softly on a summer afternoon or strongly on a stormy day. But some areas have weird regular winds that can be very strong and are given their own names. The Santa Ana winds in southern California, for example, are strong, hot, dry winds that blow from the southern California desert through the Santa Ana Pass and out into San Pedro Channel beyond Los Angeles. Shamal are summer winds that blow over Iraq and the Persian Gulf, and sirocco are warm winds that blow over the Mediterranean Sea from the Sahara desert. Other regional winds have names like gregale, haboob, and matanuska.

But what causes air to move and wind to blow? Try this activity to find out.

Materials

shoe box
scissors
plastic wrap
tape
2 small, short candles
matches (to be used only by adult helper)
adult helper

Note: Make sure that both candles are safely blown out after finishing this activity.

Procedure

1. Turn the shoe box on one long side so the opening is facing you.

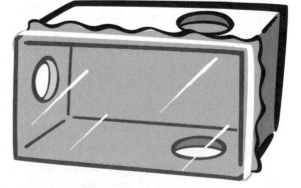

2. Use the scissors to cut two holes, one on the top and the other on the bottom surface of the box as it faces you. The holes should be about ¼ of the way from the right edge on the box and be about 2 inches in diameter.

3. Cut a third hole in the left side of the box as shown.

4. Cover the front of the box with a single piece of plastic wrap. Tape the edges of the plastic wrap to the box so that no air can escape around it, but make sure that the plastic wrap doesn't cover the holes you cut.

5. Have your adult helper light one candle and place it on the table in front of you.

6. Carefully place the box over the candle so that it fits through the hole in the bottom of the box and you can see it lit inside the box.

7. Have your adult helper light the other candle. What does the flame do?

8. Hold the lit candle near the hole on the left edge of the box. What do you notice about the flame this time?

Caution: Make sure the candle flame doesn't touch the box.

More Fun Stuff to Do

Blow out the candle near the left edge, keeping it near the hole. What does the smoke from the candle do?

Explanation

When the second candle is lit, the flame will move upward. But when you place it near the hole on the left side of the box, it will move toward the hole. When you blow out the candle, the smoke will enter the left hole, move across the box and go out the hole in the top of the box.

When the first candle was lit and placed in the box, it heated the air around it. As the air was heated, it expanded, became lighter and rose. As it rose, other cooler air was drawn in to replace it. This movement of air created a wind current that moved from the hole on the left to the hole on the top of the box. You saw this wind movement when the candle flame on the left moved toward the hole and when the smoke entered the box.

The sun's rays heat the land and water on Earth's surface. Then the heat from the land and water warms the air above the surface and the warmer air starts to rise. Because some parts of Earth's surface are heated more than others, some air rises more quickly above it. As this air rises, other, cooler air moves in to replace it. This movement of the air creates the winds that we see and feel. Since the ground in a desert heats quickly, the air above the desert does the same. This leads to the Santa Ana, shamal and sirocco winds, which all form over deserts.

Weird Science IN ACTION

The movement of air because of temperature differences gets quite complicated on a global scale. Air along the equator, the imaginary line that goes around the center of Earth, is heated more than air at the North and South poles. So cooler air from the poles tends to move to the equator. However, this movement is disrupted by the rotation of Earth on its axis. This disruption of the air movement, along with Earth's rotation creates the prevailing winds. In North America, these prevailing winds blow from the west to the east.

PROJECT 4

Tornadoes

Tornadoes are powerful twisting winds that can destroy anything in their paths. But what causes them and how do they become so powerful? Try the next activity to learn more about how tornadoes work.

Materials

2 ½-gallon (2-liter) plastic soda containers (empty and clean)
tap water
1 inch (2.5 cm) metal washer
duct tape

Procedures

1. Fill one of the containers two-thirds full of water.

2. Place the metal washer over the opening in the container.

3. Turn the second container upside down and place it on the washer.

4. Use the duct tape to fasten the two containers and the metal washer together. Use several layers of tape to make sure that no water leaks out.

5. Turn the bottles over so that the bottle with the water is on top. A small amount of water will begin to trickle from the top bottle to the bottom bottle.

6. Hold the bottles tightly and move them quickly in a small circle. Watch what happens.

Explanation

The water will spin in a tornado shape as it moves from the top bottle to the bottom bottle.

There are two forces at work in this activity. (A **force** is something that changes the shape or movement of an object.) One force is gravity, the force of attraction between all objects. Gravity pulls all objects to Earth, including water. Gravity pulls the water in the top bottle toward the bottom bottle. But gravity alone is not enough to create the tornado effect. The air in the bottom bottle also exerts a force. When you first turned the bottles over, some of the water in the top bottle flows into the bottom bottle but then stops. The force of the air, or air pressure, in the bottom bottle stops the flow of the water.

When you swirl the bottles, a small tornado forms. In the center of the water tornado is a hole. The hole goes from the top of the water to the opening between the two bottles. The hole allows air from the bottom bottle to escape to the top bottle as the water moves. As the air escapes from the bottom bottle, the air pressure in the two bottles becomes equal. Gravity is then the only force acting on the water.

When the water is in the top bottle, it has potential energy. **Potential energy** is energy that is stored for later use. When you swirl the bottles, you give the water movement, or kinetic energy. **Kinetic energy** is energy that is being used. As the water swirls from the top bottle to the bottom bottle, it changes its potential energy into kinetic energy. The movement of the water from the top bottle to the bottom bottle helps keep the water spinning in the tornado effect.

Scientists are not exactly sure how tornadoes form. But they have several theories. Tornadoes often form near thunderstorms, when warm, moist air moves upward as a cold front moves in. This causes an increase in wind speed that creates an invisible horizontal spinning effect in the lower atmosphere. The air continues to rise within the thunderstorm updrafts, which pulls the horizontal spinning air up with it. This rising air provides some of the potential energy that fuels the tornado. If this air motion continues, an area of rotation, 2 to 6 miles (3 to 9.5 km) wide is created through the middle of the thunderstorm. It's in this area that most of the strong and violent tornadoes form.

Weird Science IN ACTION

Most tornadoes begin over land, but some will form, or move, over water, creating a waterspout. These can lead to some weird phenomena. In June 1997, in Culican, Mexico, a small tornado swirled over a local body of water and sucked up a cluster of toads and frogs. The tornado then moved over the town and released the animals. It was literally raining frogs!

6 WEIRD EARTH
Geysers, Caves, and Other Strange Formations

Earth has not always looked the same as it does today. The mountains, valleys, rocks, and rivers have changed during our planet's long history.

The outer surface of rock that forms the hard surface of Earth is called the **crust**. The crust is about 3 miles (5 km) thick under the ocean floor and up to 30 miles (50 km) thick under the continents. Below the crust is **magma,** molten (liquid) rock at a high temperature. When the magma reaches the earth's surface, as when a volcano erupts, it's called **lava.**

Rocks on Earth have been formed in three different ways, giving rise to three families of rock. **Igneous rock** is formed by the cooling and hardening of molten rock, either lava or magma. About 80 percent of Earth's crust is made of igneous rocks. **Metamorphic rock** is formed below Earth's surface when heat and pressure cause existing rock to change its characteristics. **Sedimentary rock** is formed by the breaking down, depositing, and compacting of sediments (small pieces broken off of other rocks).

While the rocks themselves may not seem strange, what happens to them as Earth changes over thousands of years is. There are caves and geysers, stalactites and stalagmites. To learn more about the strange things that can change the surface of Earth, try the activities in this chapter.

Geysers

PROJECT

When water from the earth's surface flows deep underground, it will occasionally reach the hot magma below the crust. When this happens, the water heats up. If this hot water slowly runs back to the surface, you get a hot spring. But if conditions are right, the hot water may move rapidly to the surface, erupting and throwing water into the air in a geyser. While this may seem simple enough, it is in fact extremely rare. In all the world, there are less than a thousand geysers.

Try this activity to simulate your own geyser.

Materials

½-gallon (2-liter) bottle of cola
Mentos mint candy

Note: This activity must be done outside in an open area that can be cleaned up easily.

Procedure

1. Place the ½-gallon (2-liter) bottle of cola upright in an open area.

2. Remove the top from the cola.

3. Drop 2 Mentos mints into the cola bottle and stand back. What happens?

More Fun Stuff to Do

Try other carbonated drinks instead of cola. Do they work better to form a geyser? Try other candy mints instead of Mentos. Do they work to make a geyser?

Explanation

When you drop the candy into the cola bottle, the cola will immediately begin to foam and will be forced out of the bottle's opening, creating a fountain of cola. Other carbonated drinks should make fountains as well.

All carbonated drinks contain carbon dioxide (CO_2) dissolved in water. When you open a bottle of soda, the CO_2 begins to come out of the solution and turn into CO_2 gas. Usually this happens very slowly. You see this in the small bubbles that form in the drink. In this activity you created a condition where all the CO_2 comes out of the solution very fast. Scientists disagree about the cause of the reaction that happens when the candy is placed in the soda. Most think that the rough surface of the Mentos candy provides a place for the CO_2 to quickly change from being dissolved in solution to its gas form. It's not a chemical reaction that causes the fountain, but a physical change as the CO_2 changes from liquid to a gas.

Geysers work because of a physical change as well. Conditions must be just right for a geyser to form. There must be a large supply of water, an intense source of heat, and special "plumbing" in the rocks. The water comes from the earth's surface and the magma supplies the heat. Those are both easy. But the special plumbing is critical. For a geyser to be thrown into the air, the rocks that form it must be both water- and pressure-tight. The kind of rock that has these qualities is an igneous rock called rhyolite, which is high in silica and can seal the rock where the water is heated. As the water is heated, some of it undergoes a physical change from liquid to gas. Since the gas form takes up more space, it starts to expand, forcing the water above it toward the earth's surface erupting and spewing water to form a geyser. New water then flows underground and the process starts again.

Weird Science IN ACTION

The mixture of water, volcanic magma heat, and rhyolite is exceptional at Yellowstone National Park in northwestern Wyoming. Half of all the geysers in the world are located within the park's boundaries. The most famous of Yellowstone's geysers is Old Faithful, which erupts about every 67 minutes.

There are also other ways that water can erupt on the earth's surface. There is a special water and rock formation in southeastern Utah that spews water that isn't even hot! In that area, water below the surface is carbon dioxide-rich. The dissolved carbon dioxide in the water will turn into a gas, expand, and force the water above it out to the earth's surface. While not a true geyser, it does act in a way similar to what you saw in this activity.

PROJECT Weird Caves

A cave is a natural opening or cavity within the earth. Some caves are huge, and really weird to explore. Caves can be formed by pressure, erosion, or by rock being dissolved by solutions. The most common kinds of caves are those formed by rock being dissolved by solutions. These are often formed in rock called limestone. To learn more about how limestone caves are formed, try this activity.

Materials

glass jar
vinegar
chalk

Procedure

1. Fill the glass jar half full of vinegar.

2. Break the chalk into several small pieces.

3. Drop the chalk into the vinegar. What happens?

4. Leave the chalk in the vinegar for several days. What happens to the pieces of chalk?

More Fun Stuff to Do

Try grinding the chalk into a powder by crushing it between the sidewalk and a rock. Place the chalk powder into the vinegar. What happens this time?

Explanation

When the chalk is placed in the vinegar, it will begin to bubble. After several days, the chalk will begin to dissolve and the pieces will grow smaller. Powdered chalk reacts faster than the solid chalk.

Chalk is made of a chemical compound called calcium carbonate ($CaCO_3$). Vinegar is an acid. When calcium carbonate is placed in the vinegar a chemical reaction occurs. A **chemical reaction** is a change in matter in which substances break apart to produce one or more new substances. The chemical reaction breaks calcium carbonate into dissolved calcium and carbon dioxide gas. You see the carbon dioxide gas as little bubbles on the surface of the chalk. As the reaction continues, the chalk will grow smaller. Because chalk powder has more surface area than solid chalk, it will react with the vinegar faster.

Calcium carbonate is also the main mineral in limestone. A **mineral** is a pure, naturally occurring chemical compound that is found in the earth's crust. The process of forming limestone caves is very slow. It all begins with rain. As rain falls through the atmosphere, it absorbs a small amount of carbon dioxide. It collects more carbon dioxide as it moves through the soil on the earth's surface. As the water collects this carbon dioxide, it turns into a weak solution of carbonic acid. The watery carbonic acid seeps through cracks and crevices in limestone rocks in the earth's crust. The acid solution then dissolves the rock and forms caves below the surface. After thousands of years, large underground caverns are formed.

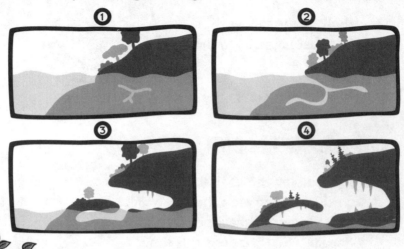

Weird Rocks

PROJECT 3

The flowing water that creates caves (see previous project) can also create unusual rock formations inside them. Two of the most unusual are stalactites and stalagmites. **Stalactites** are iciclelike formations on the roof of caves. They are created when mineral-rich water drips down from the roof and the dissolved minerals accumulate into the iciclelike formation. **Stalagmites** are formations on the floor of a cave, built up by mineral-rich water depositing the dissolved mineral on the floor. To learn more about how stalactites and stalagmites form, try this activity.

Materials

large glass jar
warm water
measuring cup
Epsom salt
mixing spoon

two smaller glass jars
wooden board
woolen yarn
scissors

Procedure

1. Fill the large glass jar with 2 cups (500 ml) warm water.

2. Slowly add Epsom salt to the water, stirring constantly as you do. Dissolve as much Epsom salt in the water as possible until some of the Epsom salt solid stays undissolved.

3. Place the two smaller jars on the wooden board so that they are about 6 inches (15 cm) apart.

4. Cut a piece of yarn long enough to reach from the bottom of one jar to the bottom of the other with a slight sag between the two jars.

5. Fill the two smaller glass jars with the Epsom salt solution.

6. Soak the yarn in the Epsom salt solution.

7. Place one end of the yarn in one jar and the other end in the other jar with a slight sag between the two jars.

8. Set the jars in a place where they won't be disturbed for several days. Watch what happens every day. What do you notice forming between the two jars?

More Fun Stuff to Do

Instead of using yarn, try different kinds of string, or even a thin strip of paper towel. What happens?

Explanation

After several days, a solid will form on the yarn between the jars and on the board below the yarn. You will get similar results with other water-absorbent string or thin strips of paper towel.

In this activity you formed stalactites and stalagmites in a way similar to what happens in nature. Epsom salt is a chemical called magnesium sulfate. When you dissolve a lot of it in water, the solution becomes saturated with the magnesium sulfate. The solution is drawn from the jar into the yarn by capillary action. When it reaches the area between the two jars, the solution builds up and begins to form drops on the outside of the yarn. While a drop hangs down, water evaporates and leaves some of the magnesium sulfate as a solid sticking to the yarn. This forms the stalactite. (To remember that stalactites are the ones that hang down, think that they have to hang "tite" to keep from falling; also "stalactite" is spelled with a "c", as in "ceiling," and "stalagmite" is spelled with a "g," as in "ground."). As some water drops fall to the board, this water also evaporates, leaving more magnesium sulfate behind to form a solid cone called a stalagmite.

Stalactites and stalagmites in nature are made of different minerals than magnesium sulfate. As mineral-rich waters drip from the ceilings of some caves, some of the minerals are left behind on the ceiling while other minerals are left on the cave's floor. Calcite is a common mineral that dissolves in water to form the stalactites and stalagmites.

Weird Science IN ACTION

Most stalactites have the usual icicle form. But there are some special types of stalactites called soda straws. In the soda straw stalactites, crystals of calcite grow downward with the drops of water. But given the right conditions, the drops of water form through the center of the stalactite rather than along the outer surface. As water flows through the center of the stalactite, it still continues to grow downward, but it also creates a tube to flow through.

7 WEIRD SIGHTS

Mirages, Northern Lights, and Illusions

Light is energy that travels in waves. The light that we see, called visible light, is just a small part of the larger electromagnetic spectrum that includes infrared light, ultraviolet light, and X rays. Light can reflect off a smooth surface or can be bent, or refracted, by other materials.

What we see as white light is really a mix of colors, creating the full spectrum of red, orange, yellow, green, blue, indigo, and violet. We see the color of an object because of the reflection of different colors. When white light strikes a red T-shirt, only the red part of the spectrum is reflected and we see that color. All the other colors of the spectrum are absorbed by the T-shirt and not reflected.

Light can cause some really weird things. It can cause mirages, lights in the sky, and optical illusions. To learn about these weird sights, try the activities in this chapter.

PROJECT

Mirages

It's a very hot, cloudless day and you're riding along a straight, flat highway. Off in the distance it looks like there is water on the road ahead. But as you drive, you never reach the water. How weird! What you have seen is a mirage. What you saw wasn't where it appeared to be. Sounds weird, but it's really the science of light at work. You didn't imagine what you saw, but you were confused by the refraction, or bending, of light.

To learn more about refraction, try this activity.

Materials

glass
tap water
pencil

Procedure

1. Fill the glass about ⅔ full of tap water.

2. Place the glass of water and pencil on the table.

3. Hold the pencil upright in the water so that the tip is about halfway between the surface of the water and the bottom of the glass.

4. Hold the pencil near the back of the glass.

5. Hold your head about 1 foot (30 cm) in front of the glass.

6. Move the pencil back and forth in the water, parallel to your head. What do you see happening to the pencil?

7. Remove the pencil from the water.

Explanation

The pencil looks broken when you move it back and forth in the water. The part of the pencil that is not in the water seems to be in one place, while the part of the pencil in the water seems to be in another.

This activity works because of **refraction**. Light generally travels in straight lines, but when it travels from one transparent (see-through) substance to another the light rays bend. This is refraction. When light travels from a more dense transparent substance like water to a less dense substance like air, the light refracts, or bends noticeably. The amount the light bends is determined by the **index of refraction.** If the index of refraction is large, the light will bend more when it moves from one transparent substance into the another.

Light reflected from the pencil appears to be in one place when it actually is in a slightly different spot. This is because the light reflected from the pencil refracts, or changes direction, when it passes from the water to the air, ending up at your eye.

A mirage also occurs because of the refraction of light. As the air is heated above the road, the air molecules move farther apart. This changes the index of refraction for the air, and causes light coming from higher in the air to bend as it moves toward the surface. What you see as water in the road is actually an image of the sky. Because of the bending of the light, the image of the sky appears below its true position. People who see the image think that the only thing that is blue and on the ground is water, so it must be water. The shimmering of the mirage, which adds to the illusion of flowing water, is due to variations in the index of refraction for the heated air above the ground.

PROJECT 2

Aurora Borealis

Since ancient times, displays of the aurora borealis, or northern lights, have fascinated and mystified people. These luminous streaks of color in the night sky of the northern hemisphere have inspired scientists and poets alike. But what causes these weird and unusual light shows in the night sky? Well, before you can understand the aurora borealis, you need to understand a few facts about Earth's magnetic field.

Materials

Styrofoam plate or other piece of flat Styrofoam (The containers under meat will work, but be sure to clean thoroughly before using)
scissors
sewing needle
strong magnet
bowl
water
magnetic compass

Procedure

1. Cut a 1-inch (2-cm) disc from a Styrofoam plate or other piece of flat Styrofoam.

2. Magnetize a sewing needle by rubbing it against a strong magnet thirty or forty times. This works best if you always rub in the same direction. You can tell if the needle is magnetized when it attracts another needle to it, just like a real magnet.

3. Insert the needle lengthwise through the Styrofoam disc.

4. Place the disc in a bowl of water. What happens?

5. Use a real compass to determine Earth's north magnetic pole. How do the direction the sewing needle points and the direction the compass needle points compare?

Explanation

The sewing needle should rotate in the water so that it points toward the north and south magnetic poles.

All magnetism is caused by moving electrons. In permanent magnets, the spin of electrons in orbit around the nucleus of the atom creates the magnetic effect. Although all matter has electrons in orbit around their nucleus, in magnetic objects the atoms are all lined up so that they point in the same direction. By rubbing a nonmagnetic needle against a magnet, you cause the atoms in the needle to line up in the same direction and the needle becomes magnetic.

Earth has a large magnetic field because of the movement of the molten magma in the planet's core. This magnetic field can't be seen but it can be detected on Earth's surface with other magnets. The needle of a compass lines up automatically with Earth's magnetic field.

Electrons (small negatively charged subatomic particles that move in orbit around the nucleus of an atom) and **positive ions** (atoms that have lost some electrons) are trapped in the magnetic field that surrounds Earth. These particles form the **Van Allen radiation belt.** When solar storms release tremendous numbers of high-energy particles, they reach the Van Allen belt, disturbing the magnetic field and causing the electrons to leave the belt. These electrons follow the magnetic field lines toward Earth's north (or south) magnetic pole, where they excite nitrogen and oxygen atoms in the atmosphere. Once excited, these atoms then emit red, green, and blue colors; similar to what happens in a neon light when gas atoms are excited with electricity, they emit the colored light that we see. This is what makes the aurora borealis, or northern lights, that circle the north magnetic pole. In the southern hemisphere, the same effect creates the aurora australis.

Optical Illusions

It's been said that seeing is believing. But you can't always believe what your eyes see. This is really true when it comes to optical illusions. Try some optical illusions in this activity and see how your eyes can play tricks on you.

Materials

2 4-inch (10-cm) squares of white paper
crayons or markers
2 4-inch (10-cm) squares of cardboard
tape
pencil

Procedure

1. Draw a picture of a bird on one square of paper and a picture of a bird cage on the other square of paper.

2. Tape one of the drawings to each piece of cardboard.

3. Tape the back of one piece of cardboard to the pencil. Then tape the other piece of cardboard back-to-back against the first drawing.

4. Roll the pencil back and forth between your hands, so that the taped-together cardboard pieces spin. Observe the two drawings. What happens?

More Fun Stuff to Do

Look at the picture below. As you scan your eyes over it, what do you notice happens to the white circles?

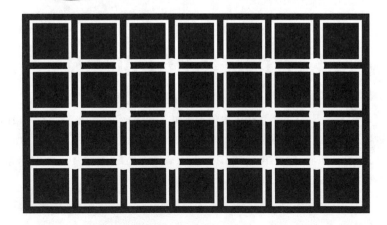

Explanation

When you spin the pencil, the two pictures that you have drawn will seem like one picture. The bird will appear to be inside the cage. When you look at the white dots, they will appear to turn first black and then back to white.

The two cardboard drawings form a simple thaumatrope. The thaumatrope demonstrates the hand being quicker than the eye. Your eye sees the first drawing for a fraction of a second and then it disappears. The next drawing appears before your eyes have a chance to react. Images formed on the retina actually remain there for $\frac{1}{16}$ of a second. The first image is retained on the retina of your eye in a process called **persistence of vision.** As a result, you do not see two separate images, but one image that contains both drawings.

In the picture with the white circles, persistence of vision comes into play again. When you look at the picture, parts of your retina are seeing the white dots, while other parts are seeing the black squares. But as your eyes scan to look at another place on the picture, there is a slight persistence of vision and the parts of the retina that were looking at the black squares are now looking at a white circle. The black color persists for a fraction of a second and the white circle appears black. As you scan the picture, the white dots appear to blink, turning first white, then black, then back to white.

8 WEIRD SOUNDS
High and Low

Sounds are all around us. Some can be soothing, like the sound of birds singing or the sound of a gentle breeze blowing through the trees. Other sounds can be scary, like the music in a horror movie. Some weird sounds you won't even hear (but your dog will)! All of these sounds have something in common. They're all caused by vibrations. When something vibrates, it moves back and forth very quickly.

Sound is energy we can hear. Sound travels from a vibrating object through the air in waves, sort of like when you drop a rock in a still pond and waves travel outward from the spot where the rock hits the water's surface.

Every sound has a pitch, which describes how high or how low the sound is. **Pitch** has to do with the number of vibrations the sound makes. The number of vibrations that a sound creates each second is called its **frequency.** High pitch has a higher frequency and low pitch has a lower frequency.

PROJECT

Doggy Do

Music is a kind of sound that people love to hear. But sometimes, the music you like is different than what other people like. In fact, your parents might think that your favorite song is just a lot of banging and screaming. You may wonder if you are both hearing the same thing. Did you know that what you hear can really be different than what your pets hear? Try this activity to learn more.

Materials

whistle
dog whistle (available from a pet store)
Note: This activity is best done outside.

Procedure

1. Go outside with the two whistles.

2. Blow the first whistle. What sound does it make?

3. Next, blow the dog whistle. What sound does this whistle make?

More Fun Stuff to Do

If you have a dog, try the same activity with your pet. How does the dog react to the sound from each whistle?

Explanation

The first whistle will make a shrill sound that you can hear. When you blow into the dog whistle, you will hear the sound of the moving air, but not the usual whistling sound. However, if you try the same activity with your dog, you'll notice that the dog will react to the dog whistle.

Sounds come in different frequencies, but humans can only hear vibrations at certain frequencies. Humans have a normal range of hearing between 20 hertz (Hz) and 20,000 hertz (Hz). One hertz is one vibration or cycle per second. If a sound is below 20 Hz or above

20,000 Hz, most people cannot hear it, although children sometimes can hear below 20 Hz or above 20,000 Hz.

When you blow into the dog whistle, it creates vibrations above 25,000 Hz that your dog can hear but you probably can't. Animals hear sounds that are outside the normal hearing range for humans. You may have noticed this with your cat or dog. Sometimes they seem to bark or react when there seem to be no sounds. But remember, they can hear sounds that humans can't.

Animal Hearing

Animal	Hearing Range (hertz)
Humans	20–20,000
Dog	15–50,000
Cat	60–65,000
Bat	1,000–120,000
Dolphin	150–150,000

Weird Science IN ACTION

Bats and dolphins both have hearing and vocal ranges beyond humans, and both animals use high-frequency sounds to help navigate as well as to communicate. Humans also use ultrasonic (sounds beyond human hearing) in several ways. Sonar involves the emission of high-frequency sound waves through water. The sound waves reflect off objects, returning the vibrations to their source. These vibrations can be used in navigation to tell the depth of the water and can locate objects that are swimming or moving through the water.

In medicine, low-intensity ultrasonic waves are used to watch the movements of an unborn child. Also, kidney stones (small mineral deposits sometimes formed in the kidneys) can be safely destroyed with high-frequency sound waves that shatter the stones into harmless fragments.

Aeolian Sounds

You may have noticed how the wind can make weird sounds as it blows across telephone and electric wires. Sounds that are caused by the wind are also called aeolian sounds. Why do these sounds happen? Try this activity to find out.

Materials

5 elastic bands, 3 inches (7.5 cm) long
10 paper clips

Procedure

1. Thread one elastic band through the middle of a second elastic band, around the second elastic band, then back through itself.

2. Pull slightly on opposite ends to tighten and form a two elastic band chain.

3. Continue to loop the other elastic bands through the end elastics on the chain until you have a 5-band chain.

4. Hook the paper clips to one end of the elastic band chain.

5. Hold the other end of the elastic chain (opposite the paper clips).

6. Find an open space in the room where there is nothing within 6 feet (2 m) of you.

7. Spin the elastic band chain above your head as fast as you can. What do you notice?

8. Try spinning the chain faster or slower. What do you notice about the sound that's made?

More Fun Stuff to Do

Try spinning other objects above your head to see if they make similar sounds. You can try a corrugated plastic tube (a swimming pool drain hose or a vacuum hose) or a ruler tied to a 3 foot (1 m) piece of string.

Explanation

As you spin the chain above your head, you will begin to hear a whistling sound. You will hear similar sounds if you spin a corrugated plastic tube or a ruler tied to a string.

Any tightly stretched wire, string, elastic band, or even a corrugated tube will vibrate when wind blows over it. In this case, rather than have the wind blow over it, the objects were spun in the air creating the same effect. As the elastic band is moved through the air, it disturbs the air, creating what are called eddy currents behind it. An **eddy current** is the circular movement of air that goes against the main flow of air. This eddy current causes the elastic band to vibrate back and forth as it moves through the air. We hear this vibration as sound. If you spin the elastic band chain faster, it will vibrate faster and make a sound with a higher pitch, while a slower spin will make a lower pitched sound.

Weird Science IN ACTION

In ancient Greece, people used to hang aeolian harps outside their homes. An aeolian harp is a box with an opening that has strings of varying thickness and tightness stretched across it. When wind blows across the strings, they begin to vibrate, making musical sounds.

Playing Glasses

Believe it or not, you can make beautiful music with just one finger. No, not by using it to play "Chopsticks," but just by making it go in a circle. Sound strange? Try this next activity to learn how it's done.

Materials

soap and water to wash your hands
towel
wine glass (be sure you get permission to use it)
container of water

Procedure

1. Wash your hands with soap and water and dry them completely.

2. Place the wine glass on the table in front of you.

3. Put the container of water next to the glass.

4. Turn your left hand so that the palm faces down. (Left handers can use their right hand.)

5. Slide your hand over the base of the wine glass so that the stem sticks between your fingers.

6. Press the glass firmly onto the table with this hand.

7. Dip the index finger of your right hand into the water. (Left handers will use their left index finger.)

8. Place the finger on the rim (top edge) of the glass.

9. Move the finger in a circle along the rim of the glass. What happens?

More Fun Stuff to Do

Fill the wine glass half full of water. Repeat the activity but this time, look at the surface of the water as you move your finger in a circle along the rim of the glass. What do you notice happening to the surface of the water?

Explanation

As you move your finger along the rim of the wine glass, you will hear a ringing sound. If you put water in the wine glass, you will notice that waves will form on the surface of the water, as the sounds are made.

As you move your finger along the rim of the wine glass, the friction created by the movement causes the wine glass to vibrate. As the glass vibrates, it causes the air around it to vibrate as well. When the vibrations become strong enough, you can hear the sounds that the vibrations create as a ringing sound. When you put water in the wine glass, you can see waves on the water's surface created by the vibrations of the glass.

Just in case you're wondering, you had to clean your hand before starting this activity to remove any natural oils from the surface of your finger. If your finger was oily, it would simply slide along the rim of the glass, and not cause it to vibrate.

Things That Go Bump in the Night

PROJECT

It's late at night and you can't get to sleep. The house is totally quiet. Then you hear a creaking sound. Is someone walking around your house, or is it something else? It could be your house talking to you. Sound weird? Try this activity to learn more.

Materials

bowl
ice
glass soda bottle (clean and dry)
balloon

Procedure

1. Fill the bowl with ice.

2. Place the opening of the balloon over the mouth of the soda bottle.

3. Look at the shape of the balloon on the bottle.

4. Place the bottle in the bowl so the ice surrounds it and leave it there for 10 minutes.

5. What happens to the shape of the balloon?

More Fun Stuff to Do

Remove the bottle and hold it between your hands to warm it up. What happens to the shape of the balloon now? Try heating the bottle with a hair dryer. What happens to the balloon?

Explanation

After the bottle is surrounded by the ice, the balloon will begin to shrink and may even be sucked inside the bottle. When you warm the bottle, the balloon will regain its normal size. With more heating, as with a blow dryer, the balloon will grow larger.

The air in the balloon is made of molecules. A **molecule** is a particle made up of two or more joined atoms. All molecules are in motion. The molecules in a gas are moving very fast. The molecules' speed and volume depend on their temperature. The hotter they are, the faster they move and the more their volume expands (gets larger).

The cooler they are, the slower they move and the more their volume contracts (gets smaller). When the bottle was placed in the ice, the air molecules inside the bottle cooled and started to move more slowly. They then contracted and put less pressure on the balloon, so the balloon shrank in size. When you took the bottle out of the ice and warmed it, the air molecules inside the bottle moved faster, and expanded, put more pressure on the balloon, so the balloon grew larger.

While the balloon (and the air inside it) can easily change shape and doesn't make any sounds, the same can't be said for your house. Your house is made of things like wood that also expand and contract but not as easily. As your house sits in the hot sun all day, wood and other materials will expand slightly. Because it's more noisy during the day, you don't hear this expansion. At night, the molecules that make up your house cool down and contract. When this happens, boards and other things that are connected rub against each other, creating the creaking or popping sounds you can hear at night when it's quiet.

PROJECT 5

Listen to Yourself

If you have ever heard your own voice on a tape recorder or a video, you know you sound different than what you think is normal. But its not the tape recorder or video that make you sound weird. It's actually your own head. And what you think is normal is actually weird! Sound strange? Then try this activity and find out what it's all about.

Materials

string
scissors
metal coat hanger
metal spoon
helper

Procedure

1. Cut a piece of string about 2 feet (60 cm) long.

2. Fold the string in half and hold the ends of the string in one hand creating a loop in the middle of the string.

3. Hang the metal coat hanger hook in the loop.

4. Hold one end of the string in each hand.

5. Hold your hands about 1 foot (30 cm) apart.

6. Have your helper hit the hanger with the spoon. What does it sound like?

7. Hold the string ends in each hand so that the string runs over the tip of your index fingers.

8. Place your index fingers into your ears.

9. Bend slightly at the waist so that the hanger does not touch your body.

10. Again have your helper hit the hanger with the spoon. Can you still hear the sound? How does its sound compare to what you heard in step 6?

More Fun Stuff to Do

Try speaking into a tape recorder then playing back what you said. Does your voice seem to have a lower or higher pitch on the tape when you compare it to what you heard when you were speaking?

Explanation

You'll be able to hear the sound of the spoon hitting the hanger both when you hold it in front of you and when your have the strings in your ears. However, you will find that the sound has a slightly higher pitch when the string is in your ears. Similarly, when you hear your voice played on a tape recorder, your voice will have a lower pitch than what you think is normal.

All sounds are produced by the vibrations of a material. In this case, when the hanger was hit with the spoon, it started to vibrate. When the hanger is in front of you, the vibrating hanger causes the air around it to vibrate as well. These vibrations moved through the air and into your outer ear canal. From there the vibrations caused your eardrum to vibrate. This vibration was transferred through your middle ear to your cochlea, where the sound was converted to a nerve impulse that was sent to your brain. Your brain is where you actually "hear" the sound.

But when you held your fingers and the string in your ears, you heard the sound in a different way. This time the vibrations from the hanger went through the string. Since your fingers and the string were touching your ears, the vibrations traveled through the bone in your head and caused your eardrum to vibrate. This vibration was transferred to your brain where you heard the sound.

The same thing happens when you talk. The sound of your own voice doesn't travel through the air and into your ear. Instead, it causes the bones in your head to vibrate. This vibration is picked up by your eardrums and forwarded to your brain. Because the vibrations move through a solid to your eardrums, (similar to when the vibrations traveled through the string), your voice sounds different from the way it sounds when it traveled through air. Your voice is different when you speak and when it comes out on a tape recorder.

104

9 WEIRD PHYSICS
Fact or Fiction?

Most of the physics that you learn in school is based on the ideas of English scientist Sir Isaac Newton. His explanations and model of the universe explain a lot about the way large objects move. But as scientists push their knowledge further and study very small objects and ones that travel at very high speeds, approaching the speed of light, Newton's explanations no longer work.

Albert Einstein was a leader in rethinking Newton's explanations. He ushered in the era of modern physics. Modern physics deals with the study of weird particles that make up matter—particles that are smaller than the protons, neutrons, and electrons of the atom. Modern physicists study particles called quarks, leptons, and force carriers. **Quarks** make up protons and neutrons, **leptons** are particles like electrons and antineutrinos, and **force carriers** are particles that transmit, or carry, forces between matter. For example eight particles, called gluons carry the strong force that holds several different quarks together to form the protons and neutrons that make the nucleus of an atom. Sound weird? You're right. But that's the world of modern physics.

In modern physics the speed you go is relative and time travel is possible, gravity curves space, and a weird substance called antimatter exists. To learn more about this brave new world, try the activities in this chapter.

PROJECT

Relativity and Time Travel

One of Albert Einstein's most famous theories is the one that says that speed is relative. By this he meant that the way you measure speed depends on your point of view. For example, suppose you are sitting in the back seat of a car as it travels down the highway with your family. Relative to the other people in the car, you are not moving. You all stay in the same place. But relative to the outside, you're traveling at 60 mph (100 km/hr). See, the speed you're traveling at depends on your point of view. It seems so simple, but it also leads to some weird things as you travel faster and faster. Einstein said that the only thing that was absolute was the speed of light (300,000,000 miles per second). Light was the only thing whose speed wasn't relative. No matter how you looked at it, it always went at the same speed. But that leads to an interesting paradox or contradiction that makes some weird things seem possible.

So, try this activity to learn more about relativity and how it seems to make time travel possible.

Materials

paper
pencil
ruler
protractor

Procedure

1. Draw two parallel lines six inches (15 cm) long and three inches (7.5 cm) apart on the paper.

2. Begin on the left of the bottom line and draw a single line perpendicular (at a right angle) to the bottom line, straight up to the top line. Write the number 1 next to it.

3. Begin on the bottom line about 1 inch (2.5 cm) from the first line and use a protractor to draw a straight line at about 60° from the bottom line, up to the top line. Write the number 2 next to it.

4. Again begin on the bottom line, about 1 inch (2.5 cm) from the second line, and draw another straight line; this time use a protractor to draw a line about 30° from the bottom line, up to the top line. Write the number 3 next to it.

5. Look at the lines. Which line is the longest and which is the shortest? Which line should take the longest to draw?

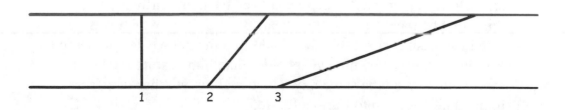

Explanation

The first line will be the shortest and the third line will be the longest. It should take the longest amount of time to draw the third line because it's the longest.

The three lines that were drawn between the two parallel lines illustrate how Einstein's theory of relativity shows that time travel is possible. Einstein said to imagine that you were on a train that was traveling along a track. You were standing on one side of the train and shined a flashlight across the train to the other side. If the train were standing still, the path the light would travel would be the same as the line 1 you drew. No matter whether the train was stopped or traveling, that would be the path that the light would take if you were in the train car. But as the train started to pull away from the station and began to travel faster, the path the light would travel would change to someone who wasn't on the train. To that person, the light would travel both across the train car and along a line in the direction the train was moving. The faster the train traveled, the farther along that line the light would go, as shown in line 3.

So, what does this have to do with time travel? Plenty. Remember that Einstein said that the speed of light would always be the same, whether you were on the train or off it. The speed of an object is determined by dividing the distance traveled by the time it takes to get there, ($v = d/t$). For line 3, the distance the light travels is longer. But if the speed of the light is constant, then the only other thing that could change is time. Relative to the people on the train, time will be longer for the person who is watching what is happening from outside the train. Time will move faster when outside the moving train and slower when inside the moving train. The value for the time will depend on how fast the train is moving.

This leads us to what is known as the twin paradox. Suppose there were two twins and one of the twins left Earth in a spaceship that could travel at about $9/10$ the speed of light. He travels out into space and returns a year later. When he arrived back on Earth, he would think that he traveled for only 1 year. But on Earth, which was outside his speeding spaceship, he would find that ten years had passed and his twin was now nine years older than him despite the fact that they were born on the same day. The traveling twin has in effect jumped nine years into Earth's future!

Einstein's theory was just that until other scientists set out to see if it was right. They knew that a subatomic (smaller than atoms) particle called the muon will decay into another substance in a certain amount of time, called half-life. When a muon is accelerated to near the speed of light with a large particle accelerator, the fast-moving muon inside the accelerator is observed to decay in slow motion, taking much longer to undergo the decay process than similar particles at rest outside the accelerator. Einstein's theory has proven true, showing that time travel, can be possible—at least for muons.

PROJECT 2 Worm Holes and Black Holes

In the previous activity, you saw how speed can lead to time travel. There is another way to change time using gravity. Einstein predicted that gravity could also slow time, similar to the way in which extremely high speeds could. But it takes a large amount of gravity to have a noticeable effect on time. At the same time, objects that create large gravitational forces also do other weird things, like form worm holes and black holes. Try this activity to learn more about these two weird phenomena.

Materials

paper
pencil
ruler
penny

Procedure

1. Place the paper horizontally on a table and use the ruler to draw a straight line 6 inches (15 cm) long near the center of the paper.

2. Place the penny on the line near one end of the paper. Move the penny along the line to the other end. This represents the trip of a spaceship from one end of a galaxy to the other.

3. Hold the paper with your left hand at one end and your right hand at the other end.

4. Move your hands together so that a wrinkle forms in the paper below your hands. Continue to move the paper until the two ends of the line are close together. Now imagine the penny traveling from one end of the line to the other.

More Fun Stuff to Do

Go outside and throw a ball up into the air. What does it do? Shine a flashlight into the sky at night. What does the light do?

Explanation

Creating a wrinkle in the paper brought the two ends of the line closer together. So instead of traveling along the whole line to get from one end to the other, the penny could travel over the wrinkle and get from one end to the other faster. When you throw a ball into the air, the ball first moved upward and then fell back and returned to the earth's surface. The flashlight shined light up into the air.

In this example, you viewed two different physicists' views of space and time. Sir Isaac Newton saw space as being like the first model, like a flat piece of paper, while Albert Einstein saw space as being like the second model—with wrinkles and curves in it. Newton saw a universe where objects traveled in straight lines unless acted on by an outside force. His flat model of space could be used to explain much of what scientists saw in the universe.

Einstein saw a different universe, where space was curved by the gravity of large objects, such as planets and stars. Einstein believed that this curved space would influence everything from the motion of comets to the path light takes from distant stars. When Einstein first put forth this theory, most scientists didn't fully agree with him. In 1919, to support his theory Einstein predicted that the path light would travel from a distant star would curve as it passed near the sun due to the sun's gravity. This theory was put to the test by British astronomer Arthur Eddington during a total eclipse of the sun when the starlight would be visible. Scientists waited anxiously for Eddington's report, several staying up all night in anticipation of the results. But Einstein went to bed. When the results were released the next morning, they were exactly as Einstein predicted.

Since that time some astronomers, but not all, have theorized that if space were curved enough—by a very large heavenly body, for example—then it could fold back on itself. This could allow astronauts to travel from one side of the fold to the other without having to travel the distance in between. Such a curve has become known as a worm hole. Science fiction movies rely on the theory of worm holes a lot because they help explain how spaceships could quickly cover very long distances in space.

The more mass an object has, the stronger its gravity. At the surface of a massive neutron star, gravity is so strong that time is slowed by about 30 percent relative to Earth time. If you could stand on a neutron star and look at what was happening on Earth, it would look like a video on fast forward. If a star got even larger, its gravity would become so strong that nothing could escape from its surface. You couldn't throw a ball up in the air and light would not even escape from a flashlight. The star would become a black hole. It's the ultimate in time travel because on its surface time would stand still relative to Earth.

The Hubble Space Telescope orbits above the surface of Earth and can see much farther into space than telescopes down here on the surface. It recently observed several objects that are thought to be black holes near the center of a galaxy called NGC4261. Inside the core of the galaxy is a spiral-shaped disk that appears to weigh 100,000 times more than our sun. Because of its large mass, it's thought to be a black hole.

PROJECT 3

Antimatter

If subatomic particles are so small, then how do scientists know that they exist? In 1928, Paul Dirac wrote down a simple equation that opened the door for antimatter. He noted that the square root of 4 can be either +2 or –2. (The square root of a number is one that if multiplied by itself will give you the number you want.) Multiplying either +2 or –2 by itself will give you the number 4. There are two solutions to one problem. In Dirac's equation, there should be two solutions, one that relies on matter and the other that relies on antimatter. Dirac interpreted this to mean that for every particle (protons, neutrons, and electrons) there is a corresponding antiparticle.

But how can these particles be seen? Try this activity to learn one way that subatomic particles can be detected.

Materials

black velvet cloth
scissors
glass jar with screw-on lid (clean and dry with label removed)
glue
blotter paper
towel
winter gloves
dry ice (available from an ice manufacturer)
hot water
rubbing alcohol
bright light, such as from a slide projector or strong flashlight
adult helper

Caution: Never touch the dry ice with your bare hands. Always wear winter gloves when touching or moving the dry ice. Always use dry ice in a well-ventilated room.

Procedure

1. Cut a circle of black velvet to cover the inside of the jar lid. Glue it in place inside the lid.

2. Cut a circle of blotter paper to cover the bottom of the jar. Glue the paper inside of the jar.

3. Have your adult helper put on the winter gloves and place a large piece of dry ice flat in the middle of the towel.

4. Invert the jar lid and place it on the dry ice.

5. Rinse the outside of the jar with hot water to warm it.

6. Pour about ¼ cup (65 ml) of rubbing alcohol into the jar to saturate the blotter paper.

7. Swirl the alcohol on the sides of the jar, then pour out any excess alcohol.

8. Invert the jar into the lid and screw it closed.

9. Turn out all the other lights in the room, then shine your light source (slide projector or strong flashlight) through the side of the glass jar. What do you see inside the jar?

Explanation

When you look inside the jar, you will see tiny vapor trails forming near the bottom of the jar.

This device is called a cloud chamber. It was invented by Scottish physicist Charles Wilson. Radiation particles from space enter the jar and travel through the alcohol vapor. When the particles collide with the vapor, droplets form and the trails can be seen. Scientists can recognize certain particles by the kinds of trails they produce. For example, alpha particles are heavy and leave straight, thick trails. Beta particles are light and leave irregular trails, because they bounce off other particles.

Using devices similar to a cloud chamber, scientists can "see" particles that would not otherwise be visible. In 1932, Carl Anderson, a young physicist at the California Institute of Technology, was studying cosmic particles (particles that naturally come from space) in a cloud chamber. He saw a track of a particle that seemed to have the mass of an electron, but the opposite charge. After a year of studying the track, he determined that the tracks belonged to an antielectron (now called a positron). Dirac's first antiparticles had been found.

GLOSSARY

acid   A chemical that reacts with a base to form a salt and water and can turn litmus paper red.

amoeba   A single-celled organism that moves by changing its shape.

amplitude   The distance from the middle of a wave to its crest.

botanist   A scientist who studies plants.

break   Process when the crest of the wave begins to fall forward.

canopy trees   Trees that grow the highest in a forest.

capillary action   A special name given to the movement of water through or along very thin tubes due to the attraction of the water to the sides of the tubes.

carnivorous   Needing the flesh of animals in order to live.

cell membranes   The stuff that surrounds the cells.

chemical reaction   A change in matter in which substances break apart to produce one or more new substances.

chitin   The stuff that some insect shells are made of.

colloid   A mixture of tiny particles of one substance scattered evenly throughout another.

crest   The highest point of a wave.

crust   The outer surface of rock that forms the hard surface of Earth.

decomposition   The natural process of decay.

density   A physical property of matter that is determined by dividing the mass of an object by its volume.

electric field   The electrically charged area surrounding something that is creating or transmitting electricity.

electrons   Small negatively charged subatomic particles that move in orbit around the nucleus of an atom.

enzyme   A special chemical that makes chemical reactions happen faster.

evaporation   The slow change of state from liquid to gas.

fermentation   The breaking down of complex molecules without the use of oxygen.

force   Something that changes the shape or movement of an object.

force carriers   Particles that transmit, or carry, forces between matter.

frequency   The number of vibrations that a sound creates each second.

gas   A phase of matter that has no fixed volume or shape. A gas takes the shape and volume of the container it's in.

gills   Special organs that let fish take oxygen from water.

herbivores   Animals that eat plants.

humidity   The amount of water that is in the air.

hypothesis   An educated guess about the results of an experiment.

igneous rock   Rock that is formed by the cooling and hardening of molten rock, either lava or magma; 80 percent of Earth's crust is made of igneous rocks.

index of refraction   The amount light bends as it travels from one transparent substance to another.

intertidal zone   An area between land and water.

kinetic energy   Energy that is being used.

lava   Magma when it reaches the surface of the earth, such as when a volcano erupts.

leptons   Particles like electrons and antineutrinos.

liquid   A phase of matter that has a fixed volume but no shape of its own. Liquids take the shape of the container they are in.

magma   Molten (liquid) rock at a high temperature that is below Earth's crust.

metamorphic rock   Rock that is formed below Earth's surface when heat and pressure cause existing rock to change its characteristics.

microbes   Organisms that are too small to see with the naked eye.

microfilaments   Proteins that act like tiny muscles to let slime molds crawl along the ground.

mineral   A pure, naturally occurring chemical compound that is found in Earth's crust.

molecule   A particle made up of two or more joined atoms.

mucus   The slippery stuff left behind by slugs when they move.

Newtonian fluids   Pure substances that have the properties of either a solid, liquid, or gas.

non-Newtonian fluids   Some mixtures of substances that sometimes have the properties of a liquid and sometimes have the properties of a solid.

organisms   Living things.

persistence of vision   Process in which an image is retained on the retina of your eye for a fraction of a second.

photosynthesis   A special substance called chlorophyll takes the energy from the sun and uses it to make carbon dioxide and water turn into simple sugar molecules and oxygen.

pitch   Pitch has to do with the number of vibrations the sound makes. It describes how high or how low the sound is.

plasma   A state of matter beyond gas.

positive ions   Atoms that have lost some electrons.

potential energy   Energy that is stored for later use.

quarks   Particles that make up protons and neutrons.

refraction   The bending of light as it travels from one transparent substance to another.

rhizome   A creeping stem that grows horizontally a few inches (cm) under the ground.

saliva   An enzyme found in the mouth used to break down starch into simple sugars.

scientific method   A process to solve a scientific question, in which you begin with a hypothesis, test it with an experiment, analyze the results, and draw a conclusion.

sedimentary rock   Rock that is formed by the breaking down, depositing, and compacting of sediments of other rocks.

solid   A phase of matter that has a distinct, fixed volume and well-defined shape.

solution   When one substance dissolves or disappears completely into another.

spores   Very small reproductive cells that are dispersed by air.

stalactite   An iciclelike formation formed by dissolved mineral deposits, that hangs from the ceiling of a cave.

stalagmite   A formation on a cave floor, formed by deposits of dissolved minerals.

starch   A large molecule made up of many smaller sugar molecules linked together.

static electricity   Electricity that does not flow.

sublimation   The process of going from a solid directly to a gas.

succulents   Plants that can store water in their leaves, stems, and roots during the wet or rainy seasons in order to survive extended periods without water.

surface tension   The force of attraction between water molecules that creates a "thin skin" on the surface of the water.

thixotropic   A substance that changes through the act of handling.

transverse wave   A wave that moves perpendicular to its source.

trough   The lowest point of a wave.

Van Allen radiation belt   Electrons and positive ions trapped in the magnetic field that surrounds Earth.

volt   A unit of electrical measurement.

wavelength   The distance between wave crests.

Index